MW00752573

CHARLES WRIGHT

BYE-AND-BYE

CHARLES WRIGHT, WINNER OF THE
PULITZER PRIZE, THE NATIONAL
BOOK CRITICS CIRCLE AWARD, THE
NATIONAL BOOK AWARD, AND THE
GRIFFIN POETRY PRIZE, LIVES IN
CHARLOTTESVILLE, VIRGINIA.

BYE-AND-BYE

CHARLES WRIGHT

BYE-AND-BYE

SELECTED LATE POEMS

FARRAR STRAUS GIROUX

NEW YORK

Farrar, Straus and Giroux

18 West 18th Street, New York 10011

Copyright © 2011 by Charles Wright

Distributed in Canada by D&M Publishers, Inc.

Printed in the United States of America

Published in 2011 by Farrar, Straus and Giroux

First paperback edition, 2012

The Library of Congress has cataloged
the hardcover edition as follows:

Wright, Charles, 1935–

Bye-and-bye : selected late poems / Charles Wright. — 1st ed.

p. cm.

ISBN 978-0-374-11758-0 (hardback)

I. Title.

PS3573.R52B94 2011

811'.54—dc22

2010054246

Paperback ISBN: 978-0-374-53317-5

Designed by Quemadura

www.fsgbooks.com

1 3 5 7 9 10 8 6 4 2

CONTENTS

A SHORT HISTORY

OF THE SHADOW

LOOKING AROUND

I sit where I always sit, in back of the Buddha,
Red leather wing chair, pony skin trunk
                                        under my feet,
Skylight above me, Chinese and Indian rugs on the floor.
1 March, 1998, where to begin again?

Over there's the ur-photograph,
                Giorgio Morandi, glasses pushed up on his forehead,
Looking hard at four objects—
Two olive oil tins, one wine bottle, one flower vase,
A universe of form and structure,

The universe constricting in front of his eyes,
                                        angelic orders
And applications scraped down
To paint on an easel stand, some in the frame, some not.
Bologna, my friend, Bologna, world's bite and world's end.

                        ──

It's only in darkness you can see the light, only
From emptiness that things start to fill,
I read once in a dream, I read in a book
                                        under the pink
Redundancies of the spring peach trees.

3

Old fires, old geographies.
In that case, make it old, I say, make it singular
In its next resurrection,
White violets like photographs on the tombstone of the yard.

Each year it happens this way, each year
Something dead comes back and lifts up its arms,
                                        puts down its luggage
And says—in the same costume, down-at-heels, badly sewn—
I bring you good news from the other world.

One hand on the sun, one hand on the moon, both feet bare,
God of the late
                Mediterranean Renaissance
Breaststrokes across the heavens.
Easter, and all who've been otherwised peek from their shells,

Thunderheads gathering at the rear
                                abyss of things,
Lightning, quick swizzle sticks, troubling the dark in-between.
You're everything that I'm not, they think,
I'll fly away, Lord, I'll fly away.

April's agnostic and nickel-plated and skin deep,
Glitter and bead-spangle, haute couture,

The world its runway, slink-step and glide.
Roll the stone slowly as it vogues and turns,

                roll the stone slowly.

—

Well, that was a month ago. May now,
What's sure to arrive has since arrived and been replaced,
Snick-snack, lock and load, gray heart's bull's-eye,
A little noon music out of the trees,

             a sonatina in green.

Spring passes. Across the room, on the opposite wall,
A 19th-century photograph
Of the Roman arena in Verona. Inside,

             stone tiers and stone gate.
Over the outer portico, the ghost of Catullus at sky's end.

The morning and evening stars never meet,

              nor summer and spring:
Beauty has been my misfortune,

         hard journey, uncomfortable resting place.
Whatever it is I have looked for
Is tiny, so tiny it can dance in the palm of my hand.

—

This is the moment of our disregard—

           just after supper,

Unseasonable hail in huddles across the porch,
The dogs whimpering,
                    thunder and lightning eddying off toward the east,
Nothing to answer back to, nothing to dress us down.

Thus do we slide into our disbelief
                    and disaffection,
Caught in the weeds and understory of our own lives,
Bad weather, bad dreams.
Proper attention is our refuge now, our perch and our praise.

So? So. The moon has its rain-ring auraed around it—
The more that we think we understand, the less we see,
Back yard becoming an obelisk
Of darkness into the sky,
                    no hieroglyphs, no words to the wise.

LOOKING AROUND II

Pale sky and one star, pale star,
Twilight twisting down like a slow screw
Into the balsa wood of Saturday afternoon,
Late Saturday afternoon,
                              a solitary plane
Eating its way like a moth across the bolt of dusk
Hung like cheesecloth above us.

Ugo would love this, Ugo Foscolo,
                              everything outline,
Crepuscular, still undewed,
Ugo, it's said, who never uttered a commonplace,
His soul transfixed by a cypress tree,
The twilight twisted into his heart,
Ugo, immortal, unleavened, when death gave him fame and rest.

———

Tonight, however's, a different story,
                              flat, uninterrupted sky,
Memorial Day,
Rain off, then back again, a
Secondhand light, dishcloth light, wrung out and almost gone.

9:30 p.m.,
Lightning bugs, three of them, in my neighbor's yard,
                                    leaping beyond the hedge.

What can I possibly see back here I haven't seen before?
Is landscape, like God, a Heraclitean river?
Is language a night flight and sea-change?
My father was born Victorian,
                                    knee-pants and red ringlets,
Sepia photographs and desk drawers
Vanishing under my ghostly touch.

—

I sit where I always sit,
                                    knockoff Brown Jordan plastic chair,
East-facing, lingering late spring dusk,
Virginia privet and honeysuckle in full-blown bloom and too sweet,
Sky with its glazed look, and half-lidded.
And here's my bat back,
The world resettled and familiar, a self-wrung sigh.

César Vallejo, on nights like this,
His mind in a crash dive from Paris to South America,
Would look from the Luxembourg
                                    Gardens or some rooftop
For the crack, the tiny crack,

In the east that separates one world from the next,

this one from

That one I look for it too.

———

Now into June, cloverheads tight, Seurating the yard,
This land-washed *jatte* fireflied and Corgied.
How sweet familiarity is,
With its known bird songs,

its known smudges.

Today, as Machado said, is every day and all days.
A little wind from the southwest, a little wind in the apple tree.

And dusk descending, or dusk rising,
Sky flat as a sheet, smooth as bedclothes on a dead woman's bed.
It's always this way at 9 p.m.,
Half moon like a cleaved ox wheel
In miniature,
Machado smooth as a night bird half-asleep in the gum tree.

———

Crepuscularum. The back yard etched in and scored by
Lack of light.
What's dark gets darker against the shrinking, twilit sky,
Hedgerow and hemlock and maple tree.
A couple of lightning bugs.

Dog bark and summer smell.
                    Mosquitos. The evening star.

Been rode hard and put up wet, someone said to me once
In Kalispell, meaning,
                    I hope I'm being used for a higher good,
Or one I'm not aware of.
Dino Campana could have said that.
Said it and meant, Lord, that's it. And please turn off the light.
And he did.

LOOKING AROUND III

August. Cloud-forest Chinese Ming screen
Beyond the south meadow and up the attendant feeder hills.
No wind and a steady rain.
Raven squawk and swallow bank,
                              screen shift at meadow mouth.
I find I have nothing to say to any of this.

Northwest Montana under the summer's backlash and wet watch.
The tall marsh grass kneels to their bidding.
The waters of Basin Creek pucker their tiny lips,
                              their thousand tiny lips.
The clouds shatter and the clouds re-form.
I find I have nothing to say to any of this.

⸻

Osip Mandelstam, toward the end of his short, word-fiery life,
Said heaven was whole, and that flowers live forever.
He also said what's ahead of us is only someone's word—
We were born to escort the dead, and be escorted ourselves.
Down by the creek bank, the sound that the water makes is almost
    human.

Down by the creek bank, the water sound
Is almost like singing, a song in praise of itself.
The light, like a water spider, stretches across the backwash.
Under the big spruce at the channel's bend,
                              someone's name and dates
Mirror the sky, whose way, like Mandelstam's, was lost in the sky.

▬

Last night like spider light webbed and still in the tall grass,
Twin fawns and a doe at the salt lick,
Hail-battered marigolds and delphinium against the cabin wall,
Coyote about to trot out
Behind the diversion ditch and head for his breakfast.

I don't understand how white clouds can cover the earth.
I don't understand how a line of verse can fall from the sky.
I don't understand how the meadow mouth
                              opens and closes.
I don't understand why the water keeps saying yes, O, yes.
I don't understand the black lake that pools in my heart.

▬

Late afternoon and long shadows across the deer ford,
Mt. Henry volcanic and hushed against the west sky and cloud clot.
Dante, according to Mandelstam,
Was not descriptive, was never descriptive, his similes
Exposing the inner image of the structure's force—

Birds were a pilgrimage, for instance, rivers political.
Cloud and cloud-flow having their way,

                                    cloud-rags and cloud-rugs
Inching across the upper meadow, now the lower.
Inside the image inside the image is the image, he might have added,
Crystalline, pristine. But he didn't.

I sit where I always sit,

                    northwest window on Basin Creek,
A homestead cabin from 1912,
Pine table knocked together some 30 years ago,
Indian saddle blanket, Peruvian bedspread
And Mykonos woven rug

                    nailed up on the log walls.

Whose childhood is this in little rectangles over the chair?
Two kids with a stringer of sunfish,
Two kids in their bathing suits,

                    the short shadows of evergreens?
Under the meadow's summer coat, forgotten bones have turned
    black.
O, not again, goes the sour song of the just resurrected.

To look hard at something, to look through it, is to transform it,
Convert it into something beyond itself, to give it grace.

For over 30 years I've looked at this meadow and mountain
    landscape
Till it's become iconic and small
And sits, like a medieval traveler's triptych,
                                     radiant in its disregard.

All morning the donors have knelt, in profile, where the creeks meet,
The thin spruce have listened to what the rustle is, and nodded—
Like coyote's ears, they're split in the wind.
Tonight, after 10 p.m., the moon will varnish everything
With a brilliance worthy, wherever that is, of Paradise.

CITRONELLA

Moonlight blank newsprint across the lawn,
Three-quarters moon, give or take,
                empty notebook, no wind.
When it's over it's over,
Cloud crossing moon, half-clear sky, then
                candle-sputter, shadow-crawl.

Well, that's a couple of miles down the road,
                he said to himself,
Watching the moonlight lacquer and mat.
Surely a mile and then some,
Watching the clouds come and the clouds go.

Citronella against the tiny ones, the biters,
Sky pewter-colored and suddenly indistinct now—
Sweet smell of citronella,
                beautiful, endless youth.
The book of moonlight has two pages and this one's the first one.

Forsake me not utterly,
Beato immaculato,
                and make me marvelous in your eyes.

IF THIS IS WHERE GOD'S AT,

WHY IS THAT FISH DEAD?

If God is the one and infinite,
If God is the clear-cut and cloudless sky,

                      Powers, Dominions,

If God is a bed and a held breath,
You have a reason, my friend, to be inquisitive.

The morning smells like Milan, autumnal Milan, fog
And a fine rain in the trees,

                  huge plane leaves stuck on the sidewalks

Throughout the Sforza gardens,
Villa Guastalla calm as a ship

            through the part-brown park and the mist.

The Japanese say we live in twelve pictures thrown from the
    floating world,
Where sin is a ladder to heaven.

             Or has been. Or can be.

First light in the east last light in the west and us in between,

Lives marginal at best

                 and marginally brought to bear.

But that's okay, given the star-struck alternative.

Remember us in the ghost hour remember us in our need.

CHARLOTTESVILLE NOCTURNE

The late September night is a train of thought, a wound
That doesn't bleed, dead grass that's still green,
No off-shoots, no elegance,
                      the late September night,
Deprived of adjectives, abstraction's utmost and gleam.

It has been said there is an end to the giving out of names.
It has been said that everything that's written has grown hollow.
It has been said that scorpions dance where language falters and
    gives way.
It has been said that something shines out from every darkness,
                          that something shines out.

Leaning against the invisible, we bend and nod.
Evening arranges itself around the fallen leaves
Alphabetized across the back yard,
                      desolate syllables
That braille us and sign us, leaning against the invisible.

Our dreams are luminous, a cast fire upon the world.
Morning arrives and that's it.
                    Sunlight darkens the earth.

IT'S DRY FOR SURE,

DRY ENOUGH TO SPIT COTTON

Afternoon, summer half-gone, autumn half-here, strange day,
Most of the grass dead, blue-gray cloud shelf
Thickening down from the west,
                                        yard light
Like the inside of a diving bell not yet in deep water.

The afternoon's got our number.
                                        If only the rain
Would come and wash it off our foreheads.
If only the rain would come, unstrung through the hard weeds,
And wash us—sprung syllables, little eternities,

The rain with its thick fingers, the rain which will fill us
As slowly as hair grows, as slowly as fingernails—
Immaculate as the Jordan, Lord, Giovanni Battista
Out of the hills, hands faith-faint,
                                        huge as all nothingness.

Where the sky disappears, the horizon spurts like a needle.
We all have death's birthmark on our faces,
                                        sometimes red, sometimes unseeable.

IF MY GLASSES WERE BETTER,

I COULD SEE WHERE I'M HEADED FOR

Autumn is over us, leaf blowers
Whine in the wind, vans wail, the heart makes scurrying sounds
As though preparing itself to start out on a long journey.
It wants to carry us with it, safe in its damp folds.
It wants to carry us, one by one.

Birds split and the ants go south.
The weevils turn in their sleep inside the red doors of the trunk.
Housefly and bumblebee carcasses drain in the sun.
Words stuttered by hand.
                    Gates of mercy.
                            Time after time.

As for me,
            I'll put on the pilgrim slippers some of these days
There, where all things are forgot.
Till then, I'll see that the grass gets mowed.
Till then, I'll check out the cloud's drift, and the season's drift,
And how the days move, one at a time,
                    always at night, and always in my direction.

LOST LANGUAGE

October, and leaves fall down. One feels the world go by.
First frost. And a licking sound
Just under the earth,
                    great wheels, or a sluice of some sort.
Sunlight thin as Saran Wrap.
A licking sound, the suck and bump of something against something.

One lives one's life in the word,
One word and a syllable, word and one syllable.
As though ice and its amulets could rise and rest us.
Whatever it is we look for is scattered, apart.

I have a thirst for the divine,
                    a long drink of forbidden water.
I have a hankering for the dust-light, for all things illegible.
I want to settle myself
Where the river falls on hard rocks,
                            where no one can cross,
Where the star-shadowed, star-colored city lies, just out of reach.

ON HEAVEN CONSIDERED

AS WHAT WILL COVER US

AND STONY COMFORTER

The longed-for is tiny, and tenuous as a syllable.
In this it resembles us.
In this it resembles what we've passed on and shucked off.
Interminable as black water,
Irreparable as dirt,
It shadows our going forth and finds us,
                                        and then finds us out.

Horizon line like a basted
                        slipstitch that shines back,
Seasonal underwork, seasonal blueprint and burn.

Last stop. End of the end. No exit.
Autumn in override,
                        everyone long gone from the garden,
No footprints, wings furled, swords sheathed.
No gears, no wheels. A silence unimaginable.
Saint Sunday, leaves in free-fall,
A little light in the west, a night light,
                                        to harry us home.

MONDO ORFEO

Three-quarters moon, last of November,

                              5 o'clock afternoon.

Acolytes of the tactile, servants of the articulate,

The infinite festers in our bones—

Sundown, and a drained blue from the sky so long,

                              ghost whispers, lost voices,

Dry wind in dry grass, our bitter song.

Our song resettles no rocks, it makes no trees move, it

Has come to nothing, this sour song, but it's all we've got

And so we sing it

                being ourselves

Matter we have no choice in.

Zone wind, wind out of Thrace were we elsewhere, which we're not,

But would be, oak trees still standing where he left them, Orpheus,

Whose head-bobbing river tongue has no stop,

                        whose song has no end.

For us, however, it's box canyon and bad weather and what-comes-
next.

It's wind-rasp.

                It's index finger to puckered lips. It's Saint Shush.

Each second the earth is struck hard
                    by four and a half pounds of sunlight.
Each second.
Try to imagine that.
                No wonder deep shade is what the soul longs for,
And not, as we always thought, the light.
No wonder the inner life is dark.
Sounding, and sicced on like a dog,
                      they all go down and devolve,
Vowel-dancing, heart-sick,
Hoping for realignment and a space that won't shine.

Unlike the October moon, Apached and blade-dazzled, smalled
Down the western sky
                into Ovidian intersect
With time and its ghostly renderings.
Unlike the leaves of the ash tree, moon-treated and hanging on
For one day longer or so.
Unlike our shrunk selves, dripping like washing on the line.

IS

Transcendence is a young man's retreat,

                   and resides in a place
Beyond place, vasty, boundless.
It hums, unlike the beauty of the world,
                   without pause, without mercy.

If it's an absence, it's we who are absent, not it.
If it's past cold and colorless,
                   it's we who are colorless, not it.
If it stays hidden, it's we who hide.

March is our medicine,
                   we take it at morning, we take it at night.
It, too, is colorless, it, too, is cold and past tense.
But it's here, and so are we.

Each waits for deliverance.
March, however, unlike ourselves, knows what to expect—
April again in his Joseph coat.

The seasons don't care for us. For them,
                   transcendence is merely raiment,
And never a second thought.
Poor us, they think, poor us in our marly shoes,
                   poor us in our grass hair.

POLAROIDS

Since landscape's insoluble,
Then loath at last light I leave the landfall, soft and gone.
Or it leaves me.
    I've got a tune in my head I can't let go,
Unlike the landscape, heavy and wan,
Sunk like a stone in the growing night,
Snuffed in the heart like a candle flame that won't come back.

Our world is of little moment, of course, but it *is* our world.
Thus it behooves us to contemplate,
        from time to time,
The *weight of glory* we should wish reset in our hearts,
About the things which are seen,
        and things which are not seen,
That corresponds like to like,
The stone to the dark of the earth, the flame to the star.

     —

Those without stories are preordained to repeat them,
I saw once in the stars.
      Unclear who underwrote *that*,
But since then I've seen it everywhere
I've looked, staggering

Noon light and night's meridian wandering wide and the single sky.
And here it is in the meadow grass, a brutish script.

We tend to repeat what we don't know
Instead of the other way around—
                              thus mojo, thus misericordia,
Old cross-work and signature, the catechism in the wind.
We tend to repeat what hurts us, things, and ghosts of things,
The actual green of summer, and summer's half-truth.
We tend to repeat ourselves.

                      —

One longs for order and permanence,
An order as in the night sky just north of Mt. Caribou,
Permanence like the seasons,
                        coming in, going out,
Watchman and wanderer. There's been no cure, however, and no
Ecstasy in transcendent form, so
Don't look for me here, incipient, now, in the artifice.

Florence is much on my mind, gold leaf and golden frame,
Infinite background of the masters—
Mayfire of green in the hills,
                      watchtower and Belvedere,
The Arno, as Dino said, like a dithering snake,
Sad swipe of forgetfulness.
Last chance, a various universe.

A few more rising and setting suns.

Always the spike of the purple lupin, always the folded hands of
   the dog rose.

Childhood, gentle monk.

His eye extinguished,
                      someone's red-gold heart-mouth has sealed his lips.

No wind in the evergreens, no singer, no lament.

Summer surrounds us, and wordless, O blue cathedral.

A few more sorrowful scenes.

The waters murmur, shadows are moist in the upper meadow.

Silence wide as a wasteland through the black streets of the forest.

Over the white eyelids of the dead,
                            white clover is blossoming.

Late snow like a fallen city shimmers the mountain's riprap and stare.

Unmullioned window, stained light.

The lapis lazuli dragonflies
                      of postbelief, rising and falling near

The broken slab wood steps, now one by one, now in pairs,

Are not the dragonflies of death with their blue-black eyes.

These are the tiny ones, the stems, the phosphorescent,

Rising and falling like drowned playthings.

They come and they disappear. They come back and they disappear.

Horizon-hump of pine bristles on end toward the south,
Breath-stealer, cloudless drop cloth
Of sky,
      the great meadow beneath like a mirror face down in the earth,
Accepting nothing, giving it back.
We'll go, as Mandelstam tells us, into a growing numbness of time,
Insoluble, as long as landscape, as indistinct.

NOSTALGIA

Always it comes when we least expect it, like a wave,
Or like the shadow of several waves,

                        one after the next,
Becoming singular as the face

Of someone who rose and fell apart at the edge of our lives.

Breaks up and re-forms, breaks up, re-forms.
And all the attendant retinue of loss foams out
Brilliant and sea-white, then sinks away.

Memory's dog-teeth,
                  lovely detritus smoothed out and laid up.

And always the feeling comes that it was better then,
Whatever *it* was—
              people and places, the sweet taste of things—
And this one, wave-borne and wave-washed, was part of all that.

We take the conceit in hand, and rub it for good luck.

Or rub it against the evil eye.
And yet, when that wave appears, or that wave's shadow, we like it,

Or say we do,
          and hope the next time

We'll be surprised again, and returned again, despite the fact

The time will come, they say, when the weight of nostalgia,
                         that ten-foot spread
Of sand in the heart, outweighs
Whatever living existence we drop on the scales.

May it never arrive, Lord, may it never arrive.

A SHORT HISTORY OF THE SHADOW

Thanksgiving, dark of the moon.
Nothing down here in the underworld but vague shapes and black
    holes,
Heaven resplendent but virtual
Above me,
        trees stripped and triple-wired like Welsh harps.
Lights on Pantops and Free Bridge mirror the eastern sky.
Under the bridge is the river,
           the red Rivanna.
Under the river's redemption, it says in the book,
It says in the book,
Through water and fire the whole place becomes purified,
The visible by the visible, the hidden by what is hidden.

                —

Each word, as someone once wrote, contains the universe.
The visible carries all the invisible on its back.
Tonight, in the unconditional, what moves in the long-limbed grasses,
                      what touches me
As though I didn't exist?
What is it that keeps on moving,
           a tiny pillar of smoke
Erect on its hind legs,
        loose in the hollow grasses?

A word I don't know yet, a little word, containing infinity,
Noiseless and unrepentant, in sift through the dry grass.
Under the tongue is the utterance.
Under the utterance is the fire, and then the only end of fire.

Only Dante, in Purgatory, casts a shadow,
L'ombra della carne, the shadow of flesh—
                                        everyone else *is* one.
The darkness that flows from the world's body, gloomy spot,
Pre-dogs our footsteps, and follows us,
                              diaphanous bodies
Watching the nouns circle, and watching the verbs circle,
Till one of them enters the left ear and becomes a shadow
Itself, sweet word in the unwaxed ear.
This is a short history of the shadow, one part of us that's real.
This is the way the world looks
In late November,
              no leaves on the trees, no ledge to foil the lightfall.

No ledge in early December either, and no ice,
La Niña unhosing the heat pump
                            up from the Gulf,
Orange Crush sunset over the Blue Ridge,
No shadow from anything as evening gathers its objects
And eases into earshot.

Under the influx the outtake,

                    Leon Battista Alberti says,

Some lights are from stars, some from the sun

And moon, and other lights are from fires.

The light from the stars makes the shadow equal to the body.

Light from fire makes it greater,

          there, under the tongue, there, under the utterance.

RIVER RUN

In spite of armchair and omelette,
In spite of the daily paradise and quid pro quo,
Like Lorca, I wait for
                    the things of the other side,
A little river of come and go,
A heartbeat of sorts, a watch tick, a splash in the night.

Wherever I turn, everything looks unworldly
Already,
            the stars in their empty boxes, the lights
Of the high houses glowing like stones
Through the thrones of the trees,
                        the river hushed in a brown study.

What isn't available is always what's longed for,
It's written, erased, then written again.
                            Thus Lost and Unknown,
Thus Master of the Undeciphered Parchment, thus Hail and
    Farewell.
It's not the bullet that kills you, as the song goes,
                            it's the hole.
It's not the water you've got to cross, it's the river.

In Kingsport, high on the ridge,
                              night is seeping out of the Cumberlands
And two-steps the hills, shadows in ecstasy across the sky—
Not dark, not dark, but almost,
                              deep and a sweet repose.

Under the washed-red mimosa spikes,
                                   under the blue backwash
Of evening, under the gun
Of mother-prayer and expectation, gently the eyelids close.

My sister and mother and father, each
In a separate room,
                     stay locked in a private music and drift away, night
And day, drift away.

I hear the gates of my life snick shut,
Air kisses,
          kisses from some place that I've never been, but will be from.
Snick snick through the Red Sea, snick snick toward the promised
    land.

Someone is turning the lights out.

                          The darkness is mine,

Time, slow liquid, like a black highway in front of me

Somewhere, no headlights, somewhere.

Hello goodbye hello. Works and days.

We come, we hang out, we disappear.

There are stars above us that can't be counted,

                                  and can't be counted on.

Gently the eyelids close.

                        Not dark, not dark. But almost.

Drift away. And drift away.

A deep and a sweet repose.

THINKING OF WALLACE STEVENS

AT THE BEGINNING OF SPRING

There is so much that clings to us, and wants to keep warm.
Familiar things—the blue sky,
Spring sun,
            some dark musician chording the sacred harp,
His spittle of notes
Pressed violets in his still darker book of revelation.

Why do they stay so cold, why
Do the words we give them disguise their identity
As abject weather,
            perverse descriptions, inordinate scales?
The poem is virga, a rain that never falls to earth.
That's why we look this way, our palms outstretched,
            our faces jacked toward the blue.

RELICS

After a time, Hoss, it makes such little difference
What anyone writes—
Relics, it seems, of the thing
                              are always stronger than the thing itself.
Palimpsest and pentimento, for instance, saint's bones
Or saint's blood,
Transcendent architecture of what was possible, say,
                              once upon a time.

The dogwoods bloom, the pink ones and the white ones, in blots
And splotches across the dusk.
                              Like clouds, perhaps. Mock clouds
In a mock heaven,
The faint odor of something unworldly, or otherworldly,
Lingering in the darkness, then not.
As though some saint had passed by the side yard,
                              the odor of Paradise,

As Aldo Buzzi has it,
Odor of Heaven, the faithful say.
And what is this odor like? someone who'd smelled it was asked
      once.
He had no answer, and said,

"It doesn't resemble any flower or any bloom or spice on this earth.
I wouldn't know how to describe it."

> Lingering as the dark comes on.

St. Gaspare del Bufalo was one of these fragrant saints,
Buzzi continues,
St. Gaspare, who walked in the rain without an umbrella and still
  stayed dry.
Miraculous gift.
He knew, he added, one of the saint's relatives, a pianist,

> who served him an osso buco once

In a penthouse in Milan.

Let's see. A cold spring in Charlottesville,
End of April, 2000—
If you can't say what you've got to say in three lines,

> better change your style.

Nobody's born redeemed, nobody's moonlight, golden fuse in the
  deadly trees.
White wind through black wires,

> humming a speech we do not speak.

Listen for us in the dark hours, listen for us in our need.

WHY, IT'S AS PRETTY

AS A PICTURE

A shallow thinker, I'm tuned
                              to the music of things,
The conversation of birds in the dusk-damaged trees,
The just-cut grass in its chalky moans,
The disputations of dogs, night traffic, I'm all ears
To all this and half again.

And so I like it out here,
Late spring, off-colors but firming up, at ease among half things.
At ease because there is no overwhelming design
                                        I'm sad heir to,
At ease because the dark music of what surrounds me
Plays to my misconceptions, and pricks me, and plays on.

It is a kind of believing without belief that we believe in,
This landscape that goes
                          no deeper than the eye, and poises like
A postcard in front of us
As though we'd settled it there, just so,
Halfway between the mind's eye and the mind, just halfway.

And yet we tend to think of it otherwise. Tonight,
For instance, the wind and the mountains and half-moon talk
Of unfamiliar things in a low familiar voice,
As though their words, however small, were putting the world in
    place.
And they are, they are,
                        the place inside the place inside the place.

The postcard's just how we see it, and not how it is.
Behind the eye's the other eye,
                            and the other ear.
The moonlight whispers in it, the mountains imprint upon it,
Our eyelids close over it,
Dawn and the sunset radiate from it like Eden.

Midmorning like a deserted room, apparition
Of armoire and table weights,
Oblongs of flat light,
                    the rosy eyelids of lovers
Raised in their ghostly insurrection,
Decay in the compassed corners beating its black wings,
Late June and the lilac just ajar.

Where the deer trail sinks down through the shadows of blue
        spruce,
Reeds rustle and bow their heads,
Creek waters murmur on like the lamentation of women
For faded, forgotten things.
And always the black birds in the trees,
Always the ancient chambers thudding inside the heart.

Swallow pure as a penknife
                            slick through the insected air.
Swallow poised on the housepost, beakful of mud and a short straw.
Swallow dun-orange, swallow blue,
                            mud purse and middle arch,
Home sweet home.

Swallow unceasing, swallow unstill
At sundown, the mother's shade over silver water.

At the edge of the forest, no sound in the gray stone,
No moan from the blue lupin.
The shadows of afternoon
                                        begin to gather in their dark robes
And unlid their crystal eyes.
Minute by minute, step by slow step,
Like the small hand on a clock, we climb north, toward midnight.

—

I've made a small hole in the silence, a tiny one,
Just big enough for a word.
And when I rise from the dead, whenever that is, I'll say it.
I can't remember the word right now,
But it will come back to me when the northwest wind
                                        blows down off Mt. Caribou
The day that I rise from the dead, whenever that is.

Sunlight, on one leg, limps out to the meadow and settles in.
Insects fall back inside their voices,
Little fanfares and muted repeats,
Inadequate language of sorrow,
                                        inadequate language of silted joy,
As ours is.
The birds join in. The sunlight opens her other leg.

At times the world falls away from us

                          with all its disguises,

And we are left with ourselves

As though we were dead, or otherwised, our lips still moving,

The empty distance, the heart

Like a votive little-red-wagon on top of a child's grave,

Nothing touching, nothing close.

A long afternoon, and a long rain begins to fall.

In some other poem, angels emerge from their cold rooms,

Their wings blackened by somebody's dream.

The rain stops, the robin resumes his post.

                                    A whisper

Out of the clouds and here comes the sun.

A long afternoon, the robin flying from post back to post.

The length of vowel sounds, by nature and by position,

Count out the morning's meters—

                          birdsong and squirrel bark, creek run,

The housefly's languor and murmurous incantation.

I put on my lavish robes

And walk at random among the day's

                          dactyls and anapests,

A widening caesura with each step.

I walk through my life as though I were a bookmark, a holder of place,
An overnight interruption

in somebody else's narrative.

What is it that causes this?
What is it that pulls my feet down, and keeps on keeping my eyes

fixed to the ground?

Whatever the answer, it will start

the wolf pack down from the mountain,

The raven down from the tree.

Time gnaws on our necks like a dog

gnaws on a stew bone.

It whittles us down with its white teeth,
It sends us packing, leaving no footprints on the dust-dour road.
That's one way of putting it.
Time, like a golden coin, lies on our tongue's another.
We slide it between our teeth on the black water,

ready for what's next.

The white eyelids of dead boys, like flushed birds, flutter up
At the edge of the timber.
Domestic lupin Crayolas the yard.

Slow lopes of tall grasses

Southbound in the meadow, hurled along by the wind.
In wingbeats and increments,
The disappeared come back to us, the soul returns to the tree.

The intermittent fugues of the creek,

                               saying yes, saying no,

Master music of sunlight

And black-green darkness under the spruce and tamaracks,

Lull us and take our breath away.

                              Our lips form fine words,

But nothing comes out.

Our lips are the messengers, but nothing can come out.

After a day of high winds, how beautiful is the stillness of dusk.

Enormous silence of stones.

Illusion, like an empty coffin, that something is missing.

Monotonous psalm of underbrush

                              and smudged flowers.

After the twilight, darkness.

After the darkness, darkness, and then what follows that.

The unborn own all of this, what little we leave them,

St. Thomas's hand

                       returning repeatedly to the wound,

Their half-formed mouths irrepressible in their half-sleep,

Asking for everything, and then some.

Already the melancholy of their arrival

Swells like a sunrise and daydream

                           over the eastern ridge line.

Inside the pyrite corridors of late afternoon,
Image follows image, clouds
Reveal themselves,
                    and shadows, like angels, lie at the feet of all things.
Chambers of the afterlife open deep in the woods,
Their secret hieroglyphics suddenly readable
With one eye closed, then with the other.

One star and a black voyage,
                            drifting mists to wish on,
Bullbats and their lullaby—
Evening tightens like an elastic around the hills.
Small sounds and the close of day,
As if a corpse had risen from somewhere deep in the meadow
And walked in its shadows quietly.

The mouth inside me with its gold teeth
Begins to open.
No words appear on its lips,
                            no syllables bubble along its tongue.
Night mouth, silent mouth.
Like drugged birds in the trees,
                        angels with damp foreheads settle down.
Wind rises, clouds arrive, another night without stars.

THE WIND IS CALM AND

COMES FROM ANOTHER WORLD

Overcast August morning.
                          A little rain in the potholes,
A little shade on the shade.
The world is unconversational, and bides its own sweet time.
What you see is what you see, it seems to say, but we
Know better than that,
                   and keep our eyes on the X, the cloud-ridden sky.

Heliotrope, we say, massaging its wings. Heliotrope.

SUMMER MORNINGS

Over the hill, the river's glib.
                        In multiple tongues,
It's got a line of talk for anyone who wants it.
Lonely summer morning. Dwarf willows,
Black corners, a safe shadow for anyone who wants it.

What the river says isn't enough.
The scars of unknowing are on our cheeks,
                                those blank pages.
I'll let the wind speak my piece.
I'll let the Vocalissimo lay me down,
                        and no one else.

———

There is out here, on summer mornings, a kind of light,
                                silky and rare,
That drapes through the evergreens
Every so often when clouds from the northwest glacier across
The sun and disintegrate.

A light like the absence of light it is so feral and shy.
A pentimento, even.
It is as though it dreamed us out of its solitude.

It is as though we're glazed here,

                         unasked for, unremembering.

It's Monday back there in the land of the Chickasaws.
The white clouds stumble upon each other, and pile up
Like mountains of faithlessness,
As clouds will, on a summer morning,

                         forgetting nothing, as clouds do.

Bright Monday. Unbearable light in the evergreens.
Dark river beneath it,

                         threading the eye of the underworld.
Above, on the great current of air,
The clouds drift on to their appointed stations, as clouds will do.

Odor of propane, nervous rustling of aspen leaves,
Summer morning unraveling silently through the woods.
The long body of the Hunter Gracchus sails by on its black water.
Late, golden July.

Time, like a swallow's shadow cutting across the grass,
Faint, darker, then faint again,
Imprints our ecstasy, and scores us.
And time will finish this, not I, and write it out,

                         as only time can.

The river rises in the mind, but empties nowhere,
Its hair naked in naked branches.
Spiders swing through my heart,
                              the moons of Jupiter turn and shine,
The river slides on its flaming wheel

And sings on summer mornings,
                              as though to croon itself to sleep.
And mumbles a kind of nothingness,
River that flows everywhere, north and south, like the wind
And never closes its eye.

Cloud skiff, like early snowfall, on the move from the west
Over Mt. Henry and my shoulder.
St. Pablo, patron of horses, appears through his wounds.
Hoofprints in khaki-colored dust.
                              Horseman salve our sins.

Summer morning. Gun-gray sky.
Rust keeps nibbling away at the edges of our lives.
Under the roots of the pine trees,
                              under the thunder,
Lightning is tracking our footprints, one leg at a time.

Bird life. An unappeasable bird life.
Saint's flesh melting into the flames below the brazier.
Sky flat and blank as parchment,
Wordless, encrypted blue,

        God's endgame, summer morning.

The secret language of butterflies.
The short shadows of those

        who will not rise from the dead.
The broken dream-cries of angels half-dazed in the woods.
The adjective and the noun.

VIA NEGATIVA

If a man wants to be sure of his road,
he must close his eyes and walk in the dark.

ST. JOHN OF THE CROSS

In Southwest Virginia, just this side of Abingdon,
The mountains begin to shoulder up,
The dogwoods go red and leaf-darkened,
And leftover roadside wildflowers neon among the greens—
Early October, and Appalachia dyes her hair.
What is it about the southern mountains
                                        that vacuums me out,
That seems to hold me on an invisible flame until I rise up and veer
Weightless and unrepentant?
The great valley pours into Tennessee, the ridges like epaulets
To the north, landscape in pinks-and-greens
                                        off to the south.

                    ▬

How pretty to think that gods abound,
                              and everything stays forgotten,
That words are dust, and everyone's lip that uttered them is dust,
Our line of discomfort inalterable, sun-struck,
From not-ness into not-ness,
Our prayers—like raiment, like char scraps—rising without us

Into an everlasting,

                    which goes on without us,

Blue into blue into blue—

Our prayers, like wet-wrung pieces of glass,

Surf-spun, unedged and indestructible and shining,

Our lives a scratch on the sky,

                             painless, beyond recall.

I never remember going out at night, full moon,

Stalking the yard in California the way I do here,

First frost

              starting to sort its crystals out, moon shadows

Tepid and underslung on the lawn.

I don't remember—although I should—the emptiness

That cold brings, and stillness brings.

I never remember remembering the odd way

Evergreens have in night light

                    of looming and floating,

The way the spirit, leaving your mouth, looms too and floats

In front of you like breath,

              leading the way as it disappears in the darkness.

Long journey, short road, the saying goes,

Meaning our lives,

                meaning the afterlife of our nights and days

During our sleepwalk through them.
The verbal hunger, the narrowness
Between the thing itself and the naming of the thing
Coils like a tapeworm inside us
                              and waits to be filled.
Our lives continue on course, and reject all meaning,
Each of us needing his martyrdom,
                              each of us needing that hard love.
We sink to our knees like Sunday, we rise and we sink again.
There is no pardon for this.

———

Bottomless water, heart's glass.
Each year the autumn comes that was not supposed to be
Back in the garden without language,
Each year, dead leaves like words
                              falling about our shoulders,
Each year, same words, same flash and gold guise.
So be it. The Angel of the Serpent That Never Arrives
Never arrives, the gates stay shut
                              under a shine and a timelessness.
On Locust Avenue the fall's fire
Collapses across the lawn,
The trees bear up their ruin,
          and everything nudges our lives toward the coming ash.

ARS POETICA III

November in cameo, pink blink.
Four fingers, forsworn from their hand,
$\qquad\qquad\qquad$ pick up their burden
And tap out the messages day-after-tomorrow licks up,
Sidereal tongue.
Gates of Mercy, stop breaking down.

Cloud strips like raw bacon slatted above the west edge of things,
Cold like a shot of Novocain
$\qquad\qquad\qquad$ under the week's gums.
Thanksgiving Day, 2000.
Four insect hulls in the far corner,
$\qquad\qquad\qquad$ fly inert on its back.
Inside or outside, a slow climb to the second life.

Rimbaud, at the end, had got it right—
Absurd, ridiculous, disgusting, etc.—
(Meaning his poems, meaning his life in literature)
But got the direction wrong.
$\qquad\qquad$ That's not why you quit, but why you keep on,
Sky with its burners damped, husk and web.

What's lost is not lost, but purls
Just out of earshot.
                    Be bright, it murmurs. Be brighter.
Words foursquare and indestructible.
The River of Heaven. River Where Elephants Come to Die.
Old lights, old destinations.

Like clouds, our dead friends drift by,
                        white and off-white, long lengths.
Tap-tap, tap-tap-tap.
Their shadows harbor in us, their mouths motion us down.
Who knows what they have to say from the far side of the seasons,
Their end-mouths so blue, so blue.

January, moth month,
                    crisp frost-flank and fluttering,
Verona,
Piazza Brà in the cut-light,
                    late afternoon, mid-winter,
1959,
Roman arena in close-up tonsured and monk robed
After the snowfall.

Behind my back, down via Mazzini, the bookstore
And long wooden table in whose drawer
Harold will show me, in a month or so,
                    the small books
From Vanni Scheiwiller, *All'insegna del pesce d'oro*,
That will change my life,
Facsimiles, *A Lume Spento*, and *Thrones*, full blown, in boards.

Made in Verona. Stamperia Valdonega.
That's how it all began, in my case,
                    Harold and I
Ghosting the bookstores and bars,
Looking for language and a place to stand that fit us,

The future, like Dostoevsky, poised
To read us the riot act.

                    And it did. And it's been okay.

BODY AND SOUL

(FOR COLEMAN HAWKINS)

The world's body is not our body,

　　　　　　　　　　　　although we'd have it so.

Our body's not infinite, although

This afternoon, under the underwater slant-shine

Of sunlight and cloud shadow,

It almost seems that way in the wind,

　　　　　　　　　　　　　　a wind that comes

From a world away with its sweet breath and its tart tongue

And casts us loose, like a cloud,

Heaven-ravaged, blue pocket, small change for the hand.

I used to think the power of words was inexhaustible,

That how we said the world

　　　　　　　　　　　was how it was, and how it would be.

I used to imagine that word-sway and word-thunder

Would silence the Silence and all that,

That words were the Word,

That language could lead us inexplicably to grace,

As though it were geographical.

I used to think these things when I was young.

　　　　　　　　　　　　　　　I still do.

Some poems exist still on the other side of our lives,
And shine out,

>   but we'll never see them.

They are unutterable, in a language without an alphabet.
Unseen. World-long. Bone music.
Too bad. We'd know them by heart

>   if we could summer them out in our wounds.

Too bad. Listening hard.
Clouds, of course, are everywhere, and blue sky in between.
Blue sky. Then what comes after the blue.

Our lives, it turns out, are still-lifes, glass bottles and fruit,
Dead animals, flowers,

>   the edges of this and that

Which drop off, most often, to indeterminate vacancy.
We're beautiful, and hung up to dry.

>   Outside the frame,

Mountains are moving, rivers flash, a cloud-scrumbled sky.
Field-patches nudge up to comfort us.
A train crosses a trestle.
Across the room, someone gets up and rearranges the things.

Insubstantial as smoke, our words
Drum down like fingertips across the page,

>   leaving no smudge or mark.

Unlike our purloined selves, they will not rise from the dead.
Unlike our whimpers and prayers, they lie low and disappear.

This word, that word, all fall down.
How far from heaven the stars are,

how far the heart from the page.
We don't know what counts—
It's as simple as that, isn't it,

we just don't know what counts.

Mid-winter in Charlottesville,

soul-shunt and pat-down, crumbs
Snow-flecked across the back yard, then gone on the sun's tongue.
These are the four lessons I have learned,
One from Martha Graham,

three others from here and there—
Walk as though you'd been given one brown eye and one blue,
Think as though you thought best with somebody else's brain,
Write as though you had in hand the last pencil on earth,
Pray as though you were praying with someone else's soul.

BODY AND SOUL II

(FOR COLEMAN HAWKINS)

The structure of landscape is infinitesimal,
Like the structure of music,

                    seamless, invisible.
Even the rain has larger sutures.
What holds the landscape together, and what holds music together,
Is faith, it appears—faith of the eye, faith of the ear.
Nothing like that in language,
However, clouds chugging from west to east like blossoms
Blown by the wind.

                April, and anything's possible.

Here is the story of Hsuan Tsang.
A Buddhist monk, he went from Xian to southern India
And back—on horseback, on camelback, on elephantback, and on
    foot.
Ten thousand miles it took him, from 629 to 645,
Mountains and deserts,
In search of the Truth,

              the heart of the heart of Reality,
The Law that would help him escape it,
And all its attendant and inescapable suffering.

                    And he found it.

These days, I look at things, not through them,
And sit down low, as far away from the sky as I can get.
The reef of the weeping cherry flourishes coral,
The neighbor's back-porch lightbulbs glow like anemones.
Squid-eyed Venus floats forth overhead.
This is the half hour, half-light, half-dark,
                              when everything starts to shine out,
And aphorisms skulk in the trees,
Their wings folded, their heads bowed.

Every true poem is a spark,
                    and aspires to the condition of the original fire
Arising out of the emptiness.
It is that same emptiness it wants to reignite.
It is that same engendering it wants to be re-engendered by.
Shooting stars.
April's identical,
                    celestial, wordless, burning down.
Its light is the light we commune by.
Its destination's our own, its hope is the hope we live with.

Wang Wei, on the other hand,
Before he was 30 years old bought his famous estate on the Wang
    River
Just east of the east end of the Southern Mountains,
                              and lived there,
Off and on, for the rest of his life.
He never traveled the landscape, but stayed inside it,

A part of nature himself, he thought.
And who would say no
To someone so bound up in solitude,
                                in failure, he thought, and suffering.

Afternoon sky the color of Cream of Wheat, a small
Dollop of butter hazily at the western edge.
Getting too old and lazy to write poems,
                                I watch the snowfall
From the apple trees.
Landscape, as Wang Wei says, softens the sharp edges of isolation.
Don't just do something, sit there.
And so I have, so I have,
                                the seasons curling around me like smoke,
Gone to the end of the earth and back without a sound.

FROM

BUFFALO YOGA

LANDSCAPE WITH

MISSING OVERTONES

The sun has set behind the Blue Ridge,
And evening with its blotting paper
                              lifts off the light.
Shadowy yards. Moon through the white pines.

PORTRAIT OF THE ARTIST

BY LI SHANG-YIN

My portrait is almost finished now

in the Book of White Hair.

Sunset over the Blue Ridge.

Puce floating cloud.

A minute of splendor is a minute of ash.

BUFFALO YOGA

Everything's more essential in northern light, horses
Lie down in the dry meadow,
Clouds trail, like prairie schooners,
                     across the edge of the left horizon,
Swallows jackknife and swan dive,
Bees blip and flies croon, God with his good ear to the ground.

Everything's more severe, wind
At a standstill and almost visible in the tamaracks,
Golden sap on the lodgepole pine
                     mosaicked and Byzantine
Inside the day's cupola,
Cuneiform characters shadowed across the forest floor.

Everything seems immediate,
                     like splinters of the divine
Suddenly flecked in our fingertips,
Forbidden knowledge of what's beyond what we can just make out,
Saw grass blades in their willingness to dazzle and bend,
Mnemonic waters, jack snipe, nightjar.

                   ▬

God's ghost taps once on the world's window,
                     then taps again

And drags his chains through the evergreens.
Weather is where he came from, and to weather returns,
His backside black on the southern sky,
Mumbling and muttering, distance like doomsday loose in his hands.

⸻

The soul, as Mallarmé says, is a rhythmical knot.
That form unties. Or reties.
                              Each is its own music,
The dark spider that chords and frets, unstringing and stringing,
Instrument, shadowy air-walker,
A long lamentation,
                    poem whose siren song we're rocked by.

⸻

An article isn't the last word, although we'd like it so.
Always there will be others,
                              somewhere along the narrow road
That keeps on disappearing
                    just there, in the mountains.

⸻

As soon as I sat down, I forgot what I wanted to say.
Outside, the wind tore through the stiff trees
Like rips through fabric.
                         The bored hum of a lawn mower
Ebbed and flowed, white horse standing still in the near meadow,

No word in my ear, no word on the tip of my tongue.
It's out there, I guess,
Among the flowers and wind-hung and hovering birds,
And I have forgotten it,
                    dry leaf on a dry creek.
Memory's nobody's fool, and keeps close to the ground.

All my life I've listened for the dark speech of silence,
And now, every night,
I hear a slight murmur, a slow rush,
My blood setting out on its long journey beyond the skin.

Earlier lives are restlessly playing hide-and-seek
Among the bog lilies and slough grass.
In this late light, the deer seem a sort of Georg Trakl blue.
The pond dims, the lonely evening pond.
A dead face appears at the window, then disappears.
The sky returns to its room,
                    monk birds pull up their hoods.

This is how the evening begins,
                    arranging its black pieces
Across the landscape.
Enormous silence, like wind, blows south through the meadow
    grasses.

Everything else holds its breath.
Stars begin to appear as the night sky
                    sets out its own pieces, the white ones.
Its moves are not new, but they are inexorable, and cold.

━━

The sun, like a golden octopus
                    out from its reef
Of clouds, or the clouds themselves, so transubstantiationally
    strange
In summer weather,
Or what's left of the evergreens in their stern vestments,
It's never the same day twice.

A poem is read by the poet, who then becomes
That poem himself
For a little while,
                    caught in its glistening tentacles.
The waters of deep remembering
Wash over him, clouds build up,

As do the shadowy pools
                    under the evergreens.
Later, the winds of forgetfulness
Blow in from a thousand miles away
And the poet starts to write.
This is the way the day moves,
                    and the sparks from its wheels.

He didn't have much to say, he thought,

> but he knew at least how to say it.

Cold comfort. Sunday,
The clouds in their summer whites,
The meadow a Paris green,

> black and tan of the trees.

Sundays are no good, he thought, Sundays are all used up.
Poor miter, poor chasuble.

Mondays are worse still. Tuesday's the one,

> inanimate Tuesday,

So gentle, so pacified.
They flutter like flames, like feathers, from the brown calendars of
the past.
Each of us has his day when the wind stops, and the clouds stop,
When everything grinds down and grains out.
Let mine be a Tuesday, he thought.

> Let mine be always day-after-tomorrow.

Everything tends toward circumference, it seems—the world,
This life, and no doubt the next,

> dependence and dear dread,

Even the universe in its spare parts.

> As for me,

I'm ringed like a tree, stealthily, year by year, moving outward.

Time wears us down and away
Like bootheels, like water on glass,
                              like footfalls on marble stairs,
Step by slow step until we are edgeless and smoothed out.

And childhood is distant, as distant as the rings of Saturn.

Let loose of my hand, Time, just this once,
And walk behind me along the corridor, the endless one,
That leads to the place I have to go.

There's no erasing the false-front calligraphy of the past.
There's no expunging the way the land lies, and its windfall glare.
I never did get it right.

When the great spider of light unspools her links and chains,
May the past be merciful,
                          the landscape have pity on me—
Forgive me my words, forgive me my utterances.

The water is saying yes and yes in the creekbed.
Clouds have arrived, and last night's moon,
                                full moon, is a memory.

The wind picks its way through the tight trees
Slowly, as though not to break something.
Marsh snipe on top of the blue spruce.

                                Nothing in nature says no.

Like tiny ghost dancers, the lupine and Indian paintbrush
Stand still and send back their messages
Through the canyons and black arroyos under the earth.
White horses shade down the deer.
Out of the dank doors in the woods,
                    angels emerge with their bronze foreheads.

And always, beneath the sunlit trees,
The easy breath-pull of moss,
                            gondolas on the black canals
Ferrying back and forth
                        just under the forest floor
The shadows of those who go, and the shadows of those who stay,
Some standing, some sitting down.

                        ▬

Duckweed lies flat on the green water.
The white flags of two deer
                        rattle across the meadow.
Transparent riders appear through the spruce trees and set off for
    the south.

I stand on the near edge of the marsh and watch them disappear.
Like them, I would gladly close my mouth
                                        and whisper to no one.

—

Wind whirls, and dust flies up in eddies.
Flowers rise up and fall,
                        trees buckle, and rise back up and fall.
Summer saddens and grows hot.

Bull snipe cackles in marsh mud.
Hawk corkscrews above the meadow,
                                then dwindles out in the overcast.
Sun back, then swallowed for good.

The world is dirty and dark.
Who thought that words were salvation?
                                        We drift like water.
Whose life is it anyway?

—

A misericordia in the wind,
                            summer's symphony
Hustling the silence horizonward,
Black keys from Rimbaud's piano in the Alps struck hard,
Then high tinkles from many white ones.
Then all of it gone to another room of the sky.

Thus do we pass our mornings,

                         or they pass us, waving,
In dark-colored clothes and sad farewells,
The music of melancholy short shrift on their tongues,
Slow sift for the hourglass.
Emptiness fills our fields,

                       new flowers rise from the dead.

The itchings for ultimate form,

                       the braiding of this and that
Together in some abstract design
Is what we're concerned about,
A certain inevitability, a certain redress.
And so we wait for afternoon, and a different weather.

We wait for the consolation of the commonplace,
The belt of light to buckle us in.
We wait for the counterpart,

                       the secretive music
That only we can hear, or we think that only we can hear.
Long afternoons.

                       Long afternoons and long, difficult evenings.

Wind from the northwest,

                       spilling over the edge from Canada.
Big wind. Many steps.

Red bug on the windowpane. This side.
                                    Nothing's bothering him.
As everything vertical outside
Bends left a lot, then less, then a lot.
                                    Red feet, red wings,
A journey beyond the wide world's end, transparent, upside down,
A kind of feckless gesture, like words
We travel back and forth to, one by one,
                                    down low and out of the wind.

American midnight, the full moon
Starting its dip behind the mountains.
                                    Fluttery shapes,
Fatal as angels in the shadowy corners of the mind,
Flatter the landscape.
Everything seems to coalesce and disintegrate
At once,
            a formal attribute of moonlight, one half
Of which we see, one half of which we maneuver not to see.

No longer interested in
                        the little deaths of fixed forms,
Their bottled formaldehyde,
We follow the narrow road that disappears in the mountains,
We follow the stations of the tongue,
Arc and trailhead,
                the blaze on the tree.

Look for us soon on the other side
Where the road tumbles down,

           curving into the invisible city.

               —

Outside, as it does one time each year,
The long body of the Hunter Gracchus sails by on the black water
Between the evergreens.

           Odor of endlessness. Odor of boat tar.
Dwindling shouts in the twilight. Rustle of aspen leaves.
Woodsmoke. Night birds. Dark linen.

               —

The morning darkens. A wind from the north, winter wind,
Harassing the blue lips

           of lupine and cornflower.
Like souls of the half-begotten, dead mosses fold their stiff hands.
The trees continue their slow dismemberment and fall.
If there were graves up here

             they would open at your feet,
The mother appearing in summer and sweet decay.

The natural world, out of whose wounds the supernatural
Rises, and where it longs to return,
Shifts in its socket from time to time

               and sparks come forth.
These are the cracks, the hyphens of light, the world relinquishes

Briefly, then stanches with human dust.
And that's what's waiting for you in the far meadow,
                    there, where the line's lunar linkup lurks.

———

The soul starts to talk to itself in the deep sleep of summer.
Under the light-flocked, mismatched spruce boughs,
It begins to know each other.
                              The lonely half looks up at the sky,
The other stares at the dirt.
Who knows what they have to say,
                    their voices like just-strung electric wire,
Constant, unhearable, but live to a single touch.

All guilt and dull ache,
                    we sit in stillness and think of forgotten things.
The stained glare of angel wings,
Radiant Sundays,
Austere, half-opened chambers of the half-opened heart,
Sun-clustered meadow,
The soul surrounding it,
                    a shimmering, speechless lash of light.

———

Dismantling the damaged bridge,
                              Crash found a water ouzel's nest
Made wholly of moss.

I asked him had he ever seen one, he nodded yes.
I asked him had he ever seen one walk
                                    underwater, and he nodded yes.
Over or under, to walk in water is a wondrous thing,
I thought.
            Then thought of Tom, just dead in a foreign land,
And wanted to be an ouzel myself and walk
                                    under the North Atlantic
And bring him back, and lay him in the stiff, mossy bed
Forever, above the water,
                        to walk in which is a wondrous thing
In either world, in either station.

                        ▬

Wind lull, and drifting mid-mountain clouds.
Shadows, like huge toads, consume themselves.
                                    Horses lie down
In the mute meadow, birds hold their tongues
As morning prepares itself for the downdraft and broken spoke,
The descent of fiery wheels.
                        God's chosen walk close to the wall.

                        ▬

Clear-cuts take on a red glow as the dark begins to shut down.
Last pass of the barn swallow,
                            last lisp of the lingering clouds.
The generator coughs off. Lights out.

Stillness and no echoes, as though a body gathered itself
For a deep journey.
Occasional flicks from the flat and widening stars.
No shank, no shadow.
Footsteps faint through the thickening trees.
And the sound of two hands clapping,

> a not unholy music.

—

Heat-quivering avenues cascade from the clouds,

> and half-remembered

Faces roll back, stripped of their foliage,
To haunt their bodies, ghost-gazed and newly peregrine.
Unshod, uncreased, the feet of the recently resurrected
Pass over the dusty passageways

> of afternoon, and leave no prints.

Out of the evergreens, one song and a bitter sigh.

How beautiful summer is,

> unclottable darkness

Seeping across the landscape
Like blood from a hemophiliac.
How strong the heart is to entertain such loveliness.
How stringent the stars are,

> spreading their welcome across the sky.

Passport stamped, the barrier lifting, how easily one is gathered.

The stars seem like window lights tonight,
                        or streetlights left on to comfort the dead
Unrolling their intergalactic curio maps
This side of midnight.
Their journey is long, and one without amenities.
Mother of Poverty, turn a blind eye on them, let them pass.

Past midnight's the other side,
                        north and south, down-ladder to dawn.
In the slick, cold corridors of the end, it is not our friend.
It's where our echoes reside.
It's what we have to pass through,
                        re-hearing each word we've ever uttered,
Listening one last time to the star-stung sound of our little voices.

The sky is hardening, color of pewter,
                        and ladles its wind
Like watery broth through the pine trees.
Who knows the heart of another's heart?
Our lives are the length of a struck match,
And our days are sure to end in a dark confusion.

Where the deer trail sinks down in the August shade of the pine
    trees,
There, on the other side of the creek,
Sapsucker off-rhythm drums
                                in the lodgepole and tamarack.
A knocking, as though he would enter,
Or exit, something
Dimmed and wind-whipped, riddled with wormways.

The blue flowers of summer
Turn toward us on their stiff stalks their sinister faces.
Something red dies out in us,
                                and closes its eyelids.
I want to become a horseman, a Mongol rider.
I want to become the black of the sapsucker's wing,
An absence of all color,
                                a feathery geography.

Chortle, and stuttering half-lilt, of an unknown bird.
They are burying Tom in West Virginia in a couple of days.
Butterfly yo-yoing back and forth above the short flowers.

White horse and mule and fjord horse
                                at grass in the glistering field.
They are burying Tom in West Virginia on Monday next.
Hum and hiccup of generator, hum of the creek.

Black dog and golden dog at large in the meadow marsh.
They are burying Tom in West Virginia, and that is that,
Butterfly back at the dandelion,

                         as cosmopolitan as the weed.

                    ▬

Like memory, night is kind to us,
Erasing idle details.

                 Circumference, for instance. Or linearity.
Astronomy starts to make some sense, and verticality.
Like sediment, inch after inch, we rise toward the stars.

                    ▬

The formalist implications of the afterlife
Seem to reveal, so far,

                 one star and a black voyage
To rediscover our names,
Our real names, imperishably inscribed in the registry of light,
From which all letters befall.

And that suits me for the time being,
Afternoon's alphabet beginning to firm up in the field,
Such radiant lettering.
If one only knew the name he was practicing for,
It would be easily there.

The world is a magic book, and we its sentences.
We read it and read ourselves.
                              We close it and turn the page down
And never come back,
Returned to what we once were before we became what we are.
This is the tale the world tells, this is the way it ends.

Low deck, Montana sky
                    color of cold Confederate uniforms,
High water in all the creeks, trees down
From wind and wet, beginning of June,
Snow yesterday, hard rain and hard frost, three bags full,
Whitecaps and white river, welcome back,
The tamaracks whisper and the lodgepole and the sough.

I slip the word in my shirt pocket: Time.
To warm it, to keep it dark, to keep it back from Forever.
I fold it in half and hold it there.
Like the cicada, however, it leaves its body and goes about its business,
Slick shell, such beautiful wings,
A corpse to reckon with.
                    Memento mori, perhaps.

That which we leave unspoken is like the hail from last night's storm
Still clustered and white
                  in the shadowy tall grass, as yet unreached by the sun.
Like unuttered words, they disappear
One by one in the light,
                crystal and golden for an instant, then nothing at all.

Like everything else not done or not chosen.
Like all that's liquid and overlooked,
                        what we don't give, what we don't take.

▬

Bullbat's back,
                high up and almost unseeable in the morning's glare,
Swallows a hyperkinetic singsong down below.
I daydream about a pierced, medieval vision,
                                a suppuration of wounds,
A spurting of blood,
One ladle, two quick and endless gulps.
St. Catherine of Siena, drink something from me.

Like the patch of late snow each one of us has left in his heart
Hoarding some hurt or other,
                        some wind chime of vague consequence,
The world has a caked and cold spot for the self-deceived,
No matter how much they glitter and spark in the sleeved sunfall.
Theirs is the dark inheritance of the doubly dead.
For them the snuffed flame, the Fifteenth Station of the Cross.

▬

Like intercessionary prayers to Purgatory,
Our little whines and our simperings
Flutter into the weather.
No wonder no answer is all we ever get, no wonder.

The purple violets are just back in the long grass.
You don't hear a peep from them,
Intent, as they are, on doing whatever it is they're here to do.
Look how low they lie in the wind,

                        how pursed their lips are.

———

In the high house of oblivion, there are many windows.
Through one of them, a light like the light
Now sliding across the meadow slides,

                        burst and perpetual.
One knows it from old frames of celluloid, exposed some,
That scorch like a wood flame, a hard light

That does not illuminate, but outlines and silhouettes.
Inside its panes the snow falls,

                        defining and flame-colored snow.
Through all the rest, no light shines,
Silence breeds and recalibrates, no waters whiffle, no wind.

———

Night fog, denser and denser.
Above it, an endlessness,

                        flight path for the newly received.
Or so they want to believe, their poor hands like poor flags in the
    distance.
Down here, however, it's difficult.

Down here, it's a different story.

                This world, no thought of the other.

We'd like the fog to drift and rise, but it hugs the ground.
Like words we meant to say, but didn't.
We'd like to tell the departed to come back,
              to say we're sorry for what we didn't say.
If, in fact, they're up there.
If, in fact, they're not still here,
              still hugging the ground like the fog, like us.

            ——

I think I'll lie down just here for a while,
                the sun on my cheek,
The wind like grass stems across my face,
And listen to what the world says,
             the luminous, transubstantiated world,
That holds me like nothing in its look.

If, as Kafka says, the hunting dogs,
At play in the stone courtyard,
Will catch the hare no matter,
      regardless of how it may be flying
Already now through the dark forest,
Then it must stay itself with just these trees,
       and their bright passage,
Those marks and punctuations before the sentence ends,
Before, in short, and black as a bible,
      the period closes in.

If, on the other hand, the hunting dogs,
      now at play
In the stone courtyard,
Never arrive, the story becomes less classical.
And the hare, however fast,
      will always be slow enough
To outlast the ending, which presupposes the source
Of story and story line,
Which cannot be doubted, and so the period snaps in place.

And thus one parable becomes another, the sun,
As it must, continues its chords and variations,

The waters lisp in the speckled woods,
The deer put their tentative feet,

                one forward, one back,
On the dead pine needles and dead grass,
Then turn like Nijinsky out of the sunlight and up the hill.
When Tolstoy met Chekhov, Chekhov says,

                they spoke of immortality, what else.

▬

Outside the outhouse doorframe, dewbows, a spatter of
Word-crystals, little eternities,

                each one of them,
Syllable, syllable, one handful of sleep, then two.

▬

The long body of the Hunter Gracchus,

                needle on Kafka's compass,
Slides through the upper meadow out of the south-southwest
As it does each year,
Ceaselessly circumnavigating
Our lives,

     always true north, the black river just inches above the ground,
Time's sluice and time's undertow,
On its way to Mt. Caribou, and on toward the northern lights.

The dove finds no olive leaf,

                so it slips back to the darkness inside the ark,

He wrote toward the end of his short, pain-dominant life.
And who would say otherwise?
There was a bird in the room, he wrote,
Each of his limbs as tired as a whole human being.
Whoever heard of a dying man drinking?

                              he asked, unable to do so himself.
And who would ask otherwise?

Late spring in the upper northwest,

                    first day of summer and the lilac just out,
Pale purple and dark purple
Over the white of the propane tank in back of the cabin.
The lilac is wonderful, isn't it? he wrote once,
Even when dying it drinks,

                    like a fish you might say.
Pale purple and dark purple,
And green of the underleaf, and green of the meadow.

                         ▭

I take down the thin book of All I Will Ever Know,
And find them, the one entry,
Three tiny words, three poised and tail-lifted scorpions.

                         ▭

Inadequate to the demands

                    imagination has settled upon me,
I listen to what the landscape says,

And all that it fails to say, and what the clouds say, and the light,
Inveterate stutterer.

                Not much this morning, it turns out,
Odor of lilac like a south wind
Suddenly through the open window, swallow twaddle
Inelegant under the raw eaves.

Kafka appears in a splotch of sunlight
                         beyond the creek's course,
Ready, it seems, to step off the *via dolorosa* he's walked through
   the dark forest.
I offer him bread, I offer him wine and soft cheese,
But he stands there, hands in his pockets,
Shaking his head no, shaking his head,
                    unable, still,
To speak or eat or to drink.
Then raises his right hand and points to the lilacs,
            smiles, and changes back into sunlight.

Late morning on the cusp of the world,
Clouds beginning to burble and build
                across the southern skyline,
Susurration of waters,
Sunlight settling like a giant bird
Soundlessly over the meadow,
           feathery touches at the edges of things.

The raven is yakking and looking for somewhere to land,
                the restless raven,
Begetter of aches and many wounds,
Malicious informant, *boia* of the airy blue.
One tree's not good enough;
           he tries another and then a third.
He's got his bright eye on me.

Under the low hum of the sweet bees,
Under the hair-heavy hoof of the warrior ant,
Under the towering shadows he must go through,
              and surface from,
Under the beetle's breast and the grub's,
The future is setting its table,
          its cutlery dark, its mirrors anxious and blank.

———

Can sunlight rustle across the skin?
Can dew fall upon the eye?
Can lamentations of the unborn grieve in the wind?
Can alien constellations comfort the sore children?
Can the hands of the dead rise?
Can God untwist all that he's twisted?
Can horizons steal our breath?
Can we take back the borrowed dust we've given away?
Can the right word ring, O my, forever in the ear?
Can a selfish song be its own praise?

———

These are the simulacra of our days,

                    the June clouds
like Navajo rugs on heaven's floor,
Gray-black in the underwarp,
Dullness of distance in the shadowless corridors
Down through the forest,

                    lilacs deglazed and past repair,
Pine squirrels riding the grub line from thicket to windowsill and
    back.

Humdrum and extracurricular,

                    the waters turn from our touch, the grass yields,
And all the spidery elegance of afternoon

Lays down its weary body,
Legs tucked and dimmed some,
                              unbidden and warm at our feet.
It's somebody's birthday, the 27th of June.
Sitting outside on the new-laid steps, I sharpen my pencil

To rig up his elegy,
Which this is, at least in part, and mine as well, I guess,
If the road he takes to return here
Is Koo Koo Boyd or Solo Joe,
                              French Garver or Basin Creek;
And if, in the Indian paintbrush sundown, the sound
He hears is the bullbat or summer snipe,
                                        then this is for both of us.

                    ▬

A fine rain and a fine mist,
                    return of the great blue heron
To Porcupine and its upper reaches, above the creek bridge.
How beautiful summer is,
                    with all its creatures and all its weather,
Sunblade for just a second, then back in its scabbard of clouds,
Robins and rain continuing to pierce and pick at the earth,
Great blue at the top of the last larch,
                              eye ready for his turn.

                    ▬

Last legs of the lilac, but here come the lupine and bear grass,
The paintbrush and yarrow stalks.
Black ants work the underground,
                        freelancing among the stones and clay lumps,
Their slighter cousins hard and orderly at the weeds.

Two whitetail does, flags up, at romp in the near meadow,
One snipe in a sexual dive and collapse
                                just there, in the marsh slough,
Moose at the salt block,
East-inching shadows like black tongues licking themselves up.

I think I'll lie down just here for a while,
                                the sun on my cheek,
The wind like grass stems across my face,
And listen to what the world says,
                        the luminous, transubstantiated world,
That holds me like nothing in its look.

THE GOSPEL ACCORDING

TO ST. SOMEONE

Reflected radiance, moon envy, we hang outside
Ourselves like bats,
                        clothed in our flash dreams.
Sunset soaks down to the last leaves of the autumn trees.
Under our heads, the world is a long drop and an ache.
Above us, the sky forks,
                        great road to the left, great road to the right.

Someone will come and walk on his hands
                        through the dry grass to the altar.
Someone will take the wafer, someone will take the wine
And walk back through the gravestones.
Succor us, someone,
Let us drink from your mouth and let us eat from your tongue.

Eternal penny, counterfeit truth, score us and pay us off.
Buried November, read us our rites.
Salvation, worry our sins.
Awake, we all share the same world,
                        asleep, we're each in our own.
Lay me down, Lord, let me sleep.

HOMAGE TO MARK ROTHKO

I tried their ways for a little while,
But wasn't at ease with them, they
                    not bringing me to the revealed.
Still, I kept on praising them.
I cast my body upon the earth.
I cast my body upon the waters,
               and kept on praising them all.
The glories refused to shelter me,
Nothing explained, nothing brought to bear.
I tried their ways for a little while,
               but nothing was ever revealed.

—

We enter the fields of memory and devotion.
Allow me, as Paul Celan says,
             to thank you from there—
Landscape, this world, this poor earth
Under the sun, holding nothing back,
This almost-nature that goes from light to light, that melts
The gold coin between our teeth,
That raises, like water, the shadow of the wound
                    up to our necks.
Allow me to thank you from all the language there is in that.

Early December, autumn's ragtag and cockamamie end.
Next door, Doctor Dave's got his pickup truck at the raked leaf pile,
Bird feeders float like flying saucers
                              suddenly through the trees,
Plaster Madonna and wood-cut edge of the Blue Ridge
Zoomed in by the bare branches.
Turkey buzzards and crows
                              drifting like lint on the Piedmont sky,
December, ragtag and gypsy day.
Allow me to thank you from all that's missing in all of that.

Form cannot deconstruct or be annihilated, you said.
The communion of saints,
                              desire and its aftermath,
Chalice and chasuble, bread and wine—
Just sonar of purification, imprints,
                              pretty tomfoolery.
Whatever *it* is, it's beyond all this, you said.
                              And painting and language and music.
Stars are the first pages, you said, in The Book of Unknowing.
Behind them are all the rest.
Form is eternal and exists unwreckable, past repair, you said.

                    ▬

In the light that shines without shadow,
                              our hiding place.
Comfort metastasizes.

Wintering in. Wintering in to distance and wordlessness.
Comfort blackens the X-rays.

                            Echoes, deep subtractions.
Wretched the body dependent upon the body.
Wretched the flesh and the soul therein.
I tried to give form to the formless,

                            and speech to the unspeakable.
To the light that shines without shadow, I gave myself.

PORTRAIT OF THE ARTIST

IN A PROSPECT OF STONE

Here is a photograph of George Mancini and me
On Hydra, the 23 March, 1961.
We're out on the breakwater.
                              An American girl named Merle
Is next to George, who's reading a newspaper. Eric,
An Englishman, and Le Grand Danois
Are next to her.
  Feta, the dog, stands foursquare and panting in the cold Aegean sun.
I'm at the far end, looking at George,
Sunglasses, white socks, and desert boots,
                                        Lieutenant's last morning.
Axel Jensen, outside the frame's edge, is up the rock-warped hill.
He's writing a first novel.
About his days with the Tuareg nomads in Algeria.
Or maybe Morocco. It's hard to remember everything.

Do I remember the would-be American novelist
Rewriting Proust for the middle west?
                              Just out of the Air Force,
He'd spent a year on the island, sleeping with some musician's wife,
Also, it turned out, American.
I, of course, loved all of this.

What else was a 25-year-old,
                    Armied and under wraps for years,
Supposed to fall in love with?
Back in Verona, that army was looking for me.
Security violation, a missing classified document.
Ciccolella, our G-2, would tell my colonel,
                    "We don't come down on our own."
Meanwhile, I sat in the almost-April Greek sunshine
Romancing expatriates,
                    hoping for my turn to become like one of them.

Mancini remembers less than I.
                    Or says he does,
Patmos just to the east, where much was revealed to John.
The winds out of Asia ride hard herd on the waves.
Narrative's narrative is seldom as slick as it purports to be,
We know, but what is this red paint print above our heads?
Ricordo di Roma, thumb smear
                    by Mary who did the oil painting
There on the wall from the photograph on Via del Babuino.
You're blocking my view of God,
                    Tom said to his ex-intended,
Camel caravans moving like Bergman across the sand dunes,
Gods bright in the bright Aegean air.
Axel dreams of his Berber robes,
                    I dream, in my white socks, of permanent leave,
And Greece, a sleep and forget-me-not, is long, and has no dreams.

Listen, memory's got a hard heart and a soft head.
Whatever light the eye sees, the heart says dark, dark, dark.
Nothing is ever lost, I once said.

                                    That was untrue,
I know now, the past a hiding place
Beyond recall or recovery, no matter our wants or our diligence.
Whatever is gone is gone,
Settling like sand dollars under memory's eyelid,
Down to the darkness where nothing stirs,

                                    nothing except the heart,
That eyeless fish, drifting on slow, invisible currents
Beneath a blue hopscotch of islands where,

                                    up above,
Somebody young and undiminished assembles a few friends
Along a breakwater in the sun.

                          Then one of them takes a camera out.

ROSSO VENEXIANO

And here is a photograph of me taking a photograph
Of Holly and me. In 1969, I think,
In Venice,
        Timothy Hennessey's wretched painting
Behind us, the ornate Venetian mirror throwing us back
Spotted, rejuvenate, shelved in two.

And that's not half bad, I'd say,
Chihuly downstairs, and Luke Hodgkin, *acqua alta*
Finally out the door,
                the schifo from the trattoria
Flushed through the ground floor hallway's side rooms,
The lettuce flats and cardboard wine boxes
                        sucked back toward Malamocco.

End of March, thirty-three years ago.
Across the water, in S. Sebastiano, the Veronesi
Are arc-lit and scaffolded,
The *Phantom Turk*, square-rigged ghost ship,
                      still moored on the Grand Canal
In front of Palazzo Guggenheim.

Or so we imagined it,
                Corvo at large on the damp streets,

Pound on his daily constitutional, as I've said before,
Exhuming the Zattere and Innocenti,
Fluttering candlelike guttering light
At night in the windows high up in Palazzo Barbaro.

Our altered and unreal lives.

                  How silly it all was, how delicious,
Palazzo this and Palazzo that,
Guardi and Canaletto from every bridge and opening,
The gold-domed Dogana a harsh relief in the winter sun.
Nobody sat on the steps that year,

                        not I, not anyone.

What else is bereft in the camera's lens, or the mirror's eye?
People, of course, and the future; Campo S. Polo:
Sabo, co fa scuro, Gran Balo Macabro, the poster announced.
Lord, the detritus.

               Write, the voice said. *For whom?* came the response.
For the dead whom thou didst love, came the instant reply.

And will they read me?
Aye, for they return as posterity, the voice answered one last time.
Red of Titian's *Assumption*, red of the Doge's fingernail,
Blood red of the Serenissima,
Lagoon light, sunset and cloud blaze,

                  red of the Cardinal entourage.

ARRIVEDERCI KINGSPORT

It's all Interstate anymore,
                              the sedge fields Ted Glynn and I
Would shoot doves on. Or underwater.
The Country Music Highway, out of the hollers and backwash
Of southeastern Kentucky, old U.S. 23,
Has carried the boys to a different demarcation,
Their voices like field mice in the 21st-century wind.

Goodbye to that stuff,
The late '40s and early '50s and adolescence,
Dolores Urquiza and Clara Hall
                              —memory's music just out of tune—
Drifting in their 7th-grade frocks across the Civic Auditorium floor.
Goodbye to Sundays, and band practice,
                                        the backseats of cars,
Goodbye to WKPT and everybody's song.

Jesus, it's all still a fist of mist
That keeps on cleaning my clock,
                              tick-tock, my youth, tick-tock, my youth,
Everything going away again and again toward the light.
Who will remember Christina Marsh and Bobby Step,
                                        now that I'm gone?
Who will remember the frog famine,

Now that the nameless roads

                    have carried us all from town?

Midsummer in 1951,

               the censer gone,

The call-and-response both gone, how far away is that?

A life unremarkable, but one which was remarked,

It turns out. Without consolation, it seemed,

                       adolescence,

The summer seeped to its end,

The sweet smoke of the past like bandages

                  on all our imagined wounds.

And once upon a time, in the long afternoons of autumn,

The boys and girls would lay them down

                 in the bitter weeds

And watch the hidden meanderings

Of stars in their luminous disguise,

              that ill-invested blue.

Is there reprieve for this act?

Is there reprieve for such regard?

                Not in this life, and not in the next.

Well, yes, but beside the point.

And what is the point?

            The point is the drawn-out landfall

From Chestnut Ridge to Moccasin Gap.

The point is U.S. 11W disappearing

In front of us and behind our backs,

                         the winter winds
And the clouds that dog our footsteps, out west and back east.

And so the dance continues,
Boots Duke and Jackie Imray,

                         Bevo and Kay Churchill,
Jim Churchill and Nancy Sims,
Name after name dropping into the dark waters of day-before-
    yesterday.
Champe Bachelder and Karen Beall,

                         Bill Ring and Sarah Lou,
Slow dance, the music coming up again.

Goodnight, sweetheart, well, it's time to go.
Ta-ta-ta-ta-tum, Goodnight, sweetheart, well, it's time to go,
                         the soft-aired Tennessee night
Gathers its children in its cupped hands.
Time has its covenant, and who's to say that it is unjust.
We make our sad arrangements.

                         The sky clears, the sun sets.
No matter the words, we never forget our own song.

A cold draft blows steadily from a crack in the window jamb.
It's good for the soul.
For some reason, I think of monuments in the high desert,
                     and what dissembles them.

We're all born with a one-way ticket, of course,
Thus do we take our deaths up on our shoulders and walk and walk,
Trying to get back.

We'd like to move as the water moves.
We'd like to cover the earth
                  the way the wind covers the earth.
We'd like to burn our way there, like fire.

It's not in the cards.
Uncertainty harbors us like winter mist—
                  the further we go, the deeper it gets.
Sundown now, and wind from the northwest.

The month is abandoned.
                  Volvos go wandering to and fro
Like lost polar bears. The landscape is simple and brown.
The future's behind us, panting, lolling its black tongue.

Sun-sliding morning. The doors of the world stand open,
The one up and the one down.
                    Twice-blessed by their golden handles,
We try them both, but they don't open, not yet, they don't open.

Wind from the west as usual,
                    harp-limbs of bare trees
In southwest corner of things.
The music of memory has its own pitch,
                    which not everyone hears.

Cloud-gondolas floating in with the east-moving wind-waters,
Black-hulled and gilt-edged,
                    white on white up above, smooth pole.
Later, the sunset, flamingo, great bird of passage.

Dry autumn and dry winter, dry spring.
The nights drift over us,
                    spun toward the iron Atlantic.
Memory's mantras hum like electric lights in their slow flow.

Bits, and small bits, and pieces of things.
Memory has its own affections,

                        bleak, unappointed rounds,
High beams in the dark driveway, no one behind the wheel.

IN PRAISE OF

THOMAS CHATTERTON

Humdrum of helicopter dwindling off to the west,
Full moon in a night or two.
Why do I think of Chatterton, *the marvellous boy*,
Just seventeen and under the hill over two hundred years ago?
Is it the bulge of the moon?
                    Is it the double consonant of wind and the weather?

Both Keats and Wordsworth thought well of him.
The purest English, I think, is Chatterton's Keats wrote
In a letter to George in Louisville, Kentucky.
Wordsworth referred to him as *the sleepless soul that perished in*
    his pride,
Inventing his own vocabulary, dead by his own hand.

I remember seeing a picture once, an inked engraving, I think,
Of Chatterton as a suicide,
Sprawled on his bed, gargoyles and fanged, feathery creatures
Circling above him.
Outside the window, a moon like this one.
                    God rest him, *and happie bee hys dolle*.

SATURDAY AFTERNOON

The sadness of sunlight lies like fine dust on the evergreens.
Even the wind can't move it,
The wind that settles across the afternoon like a luck-hungry bird,
Reshuffling its feathers from time to time,
                        and cricking its claws.
The slow sleep and sad shine of sunlight.

Shadows are clumsy and crude, their eggs few,
And dragonflies, like lumescent Ohio Blue Tip matchsticks,
Puzzle the part-opened iris stalks,
                        hovering and stiff.
New flies frenetic against the glass,
Woodpeckers at their clocks,
                  the horses ablaze in the grained light.

Although the lilac is long dead, the bees still seek its entrance.
In vain, the chilled and resurgent bees.
It's not so much the lilac they want
As subtraction of lilac,
               some sumptuous, idyllic door
Unlatching to them its inner and sumptuous rooms.

The season, however, outlegs them,
Unanswerable in its instruments
                    and its empty cells.
And bees must follow it willy-nilly, and lockstep,
Right down the air, where the world reloads
                    and offers up
Its lesser mansions, its smaller rooms.

This is no metaphor, this is the way it just is,
Creaking of wheels endemic under the earth,
                    slick pistil and piston,
Pulleys raising the platforms up, and pulling them down.
We walk on the roofs of great houses,
                    some of them quick, some not,
All of them turning like a river, all of them ours.

WEDNESDAY MORNING

There is a stillness across the morning,
                     sudden absence of something,
Horses escaped, birds mum, the wind that has stopped blowing.
The strict vocabulary of the dead has a word for it,
This stillness, that still escapes us
                     like breath, like grain through our fingers.
But like the birds, they are mum.
And like the horses, and like the wind,
                     they stay that way.

For the time being, at least.
At least until the dead come back, and both the horses do, and
    the birds.
At least until the morning recovers her balance,
And rises,
               up from her one elbow,
Her blue hand on her blue hip,
And parcels herself into a luminance, and sings.

Until then, we mull it and mark its dark erasures.
The trees go on holding their arms out.
The sunlight, with its ship's code
Stealthily signaling from water to willow leaf and back,

Explains it once and for all,
But we can see nothing, or take in nothing, it is so still.

There is a stillness in us, too,
                    a different stillness, one like a light's flash
From one end of a grain of sand to the other end,
Tiny, that longs to impose itself on our vague solitude,
And on our incumbent lives.
Essential stillness at the center of things,
                                        the stillness of stones,
Stillness of all that we do not do, that we are not.

It's not, as I say, the same story,
Pointillist array of yellowweed unmovable
In the far meadow.
                    But look,
A breath from the blue lady, a bend in the long-legged grass,
The stillness beginning to grow small,
                                        and smaller still,
Until it is overgrown, and hidden, as ours is.

HOMAGE TO GIORGIO MORANDI

You, of all the masters, have been the secret sharer
Of what's most important,
                              exclusion,
Until the form is given us out of what has been given,
And never imposed upon,
Scrape and erase, scrape and erase
                                        until the object comes clear.

I well remember the time I didn't visit you
In Bologna, 1964,
                    the year you died.
Bob Koffler and Wolf Kahn went, Mary and all the rest of us
Remaining in Rome. What a mistake.
The next thing we heard was your *coccodrillo* in *The Daily
    American.*

And now you've become iconic, as only is right,
Grizzano and atelier,
                        permanent as a pair of finger rings
On your worldwide hands.
The farther out of the picture you go, the greater it grows.
The farther out of our lives you go, *la stessa storia.*

And now you have become an eternal occasion.
The less in view, the more your presence
Surrounds us,
                    and concentrates our tick-tock attention.
How proper it is we see you most where you are not,
Among your objects.
                              This bottle, for instance, this vase.

Bologna made you and Bologna undid you in the scheme of things.
It never mattered to you.
How little we knew about your life,
                              how little we knew about anything,
The Roman nights so florid and opposite of all that you stood for.
We bathed in our own dark waters,
                              you dabbled your brush in yours.

The would-be artist's credo—
He keeps to himself
                    and doesn't play well with others—
Found short shrift on your star chart.
Still, no serious time for anything but your work,
You looked as hard as anyone ever looked,
                              then left it out.

LITTLE APOCALYPSE

The butterfly's out on noon patrol,
                    dragoning down to the rapt flower heads.
The ground shudders beneath the ant's hoof.
Under cover of sunlight, the dung beetle bores through his
    summer dreams.
High up, in another world,
                    the clouds assemble and mumble their messages.
Sedate, avaricious life,

The earthworm huddled in darkness,
                    the robin, great warrior, above,
Reworking across the shattered graves of his fathers.
The grass, in its green time, bows to whatever moves it.
Afternoon's ready to shove its spade
                    deep in the dirt,
Coffins and sugar bones awash in the sudden sun.

Inside the basements of the world,
                    the clear-out's begun,
Lightning around the thunder-throat of the underearth,
A drop of fire and a drop of fire,
Bright bandages of fog
                    starting to comfort the aftermath.
Then, from the black horizon, four horses heave up, flash on their
    faces.

MY OWN LITTLE CIVIL WAR

I come from the only county in Tennessee that did not secede
Throughout the entire Civil War,
                Sullivan County,
Rock-ribbed, recalcitrant, Appalachian cornerstone.
My kinfolk were otherwise,
Arkansans and Mississippians,
                    Virginians and Tarheels.
Still, I was born just a half mile from Shiloh churchyard,
And had a relative, the family story goes, who served there,
Confederate quartermaster,
                   who took the occasion, that first day,
To liberate many bills
From Union coffers as the Johnnys swept through to the river,
And never replaced them when the Bluebellies swept back
And through the following afternoon.

My great-grandfather Wright left VMI to join up
With Lee and the Army of Northern Virginia
Somewhere near Richmond,
                and ended up,
Lucky lad, a staff officer in the general's command.
Who knows how many letters that took?
After the war he went back to Lexington, with Lee,

The general to Washington College and immortality,
Capt. Wright at the far end of town,
                            still marching away the lost cause.
Marse Robert has his horse and white tomb
Under the oak trees.
My great-grandfather has his name in a long thin line
Of others who were captains of the Corps of Cadets,
                                   too little, boys, too late.

My great-grandfather Penzel, four years in the country,
Saddled up in 1861 in Little Rock
With the Capital City Guards
                         and struck out for Tennessee.
His name is last on the list, carved in print on an obelisk,
In front of a civic building somewhere near downtown.
Like just about everyone else, he finished the war as a captain,
Enduring the raw campaigns
                       of southeast Tennessee,
Chickamauga, two years in Rock Island prison, deep
Wounds in his mouth and elsewhere,
Then back, like all the others, into the thick of it.
A long way for a country boy,
                       slaveless, and no stake in it,
From the green hills of Bohemia.

There are letters from Isaac Wright,
                       Bladen County, North Carolina,

1856,
To his son near Lafayette Courthouse, Red River, Arkansas,
A dozen or so, I cannot decipher.

                        Political
And familial, about President Franklin Pierce,
Wishing that John C. Calhoun

                        were still alive and president
Instead, and the Constitutional rights of the South
Established with greater force,

                        and greater clarity.
"I fear that we shall yet have difficulties with our Northern Brethren."
And then the price of negroes,
Nearby farms, the fear of high water,

                        the price of cotton, always the price of cotton.
Then "love to Elizabeth, my son, and you and the children."

All this from the documents

                        left by my great-aunt Marcella,
A folder that also holds,
Inexplicably, my grandmother's marriage license
And one short sketch, so titled, of the Fulton and Nowland families.
So much for all that . . .

                        However, wrapped in wax paper,
Among the letters, is another small envelope
Containing a lock, so called,

                        of Robert E. Lee's hair,
Sent by him to the wife of the lucky lad from VMI . . .

That's it, my own little Civil War—

                      a lock of hair,

A dozen unreadable letters,

An obit or two,

And half the weight and half-life

                      of a half-healed and hurting world.

LA DOLCEAMARA VITA

Autumn is over. The winter rains
Have settled like feathers from wild geese
                                        deep in the trees.

I start my afternoon rote walk, the wet-step and weekend one,
Up Locust Avenue and back down.

The cold-eaten, sap-sunken gold of the maple leaves
Takes in the light and grows big,

The church chimes like empty villages,
                                        ruin-riddled, far away,
Where nobody goes.

The dogwood is redder now than summer's chokecherry,
Sunset sheen like old wax on the steps into the sky,

Rainwater gone, drifting under the streets while nobody notices.
I reach the hospital and turn back.

Behind me, day darkens, in front of me darker still.
If I had it all to do over again, I'd pull the light

Toward me and start to gleam,

              and then not gleam, the way the leaves do,
The dying leaves, and the cold flowers.

SUN-SADDLED, COKE-COPPING,

BAD-BOOZING BLUES

Front porch of the first cabin, with Luke.
July, most likely, and damp, both of us wearing rubber boots.
Just out of the photograph, beyond the toe of my left foot,
The railing where Tim and I, one afternoon,

                         carved our poor initials
While working on verses for his song, "Stockman's Bar Again, Boys."
Both song and singer are gone now, and the railing too.

We all sang in the chorus

                    back in L.A., in the recording studio,
Holly and I and Bill Myers and Kelly and Johnny Rubinstein.
Such joyful music, so long ago,

                    before the coke crash and the whiskey blows.
Sun-soured Montana daydreams,
Los Angeles and its dark snood so soft on the neck.
Lie still I'm working on it lie still.

Billy Mitchell's just come by, somebody stole his tools,
Leland Driggs has shot an elk and broke the county's rules.
Sweet Dan Kelly's on his Cat, watch out and back away,

Snuffy Bruns is feeding squirrels and Crash is bucking hay.
Big John Phelan's got outside a half a fifth of gin,
We've all gone and gotten drunk in Stockman's Bar again.

Dead frequency, Slick, over and out.
It's mostly a matter of what kind of noise you make.
American Hot Wax, for instance, and "Stand by Your Man"—
                              George Jones, type-casting for sure.
And music, always music—keyboard and guitar, violin,
Anything with a string.
                    Your band was called Fun Zone, you up front,
Poncher on drums, Wolfie on bass, and Johnny R. at the piano.

And others. Until the lights went out.
                              Renaissance boy,
With coke up your nose and marijuana in your eye,
We loved you the best we could, but nobody loved you enough.
Except Miss Whiskey.
You roll in your sweet baby's arms now, as once you said you would,
And lay your body down,
                    in your meadow, in the mountains, all alone.

—TIM McINTIRE (1944–1986)

IN PRAISE OF HAN SHAN

Cold Mountain and Cold Mountain became the same thing in the
   mind,
The first last seen
                 slipping into a crevice in the second.

Only the poems remained,
                 scrawled on the rocks and trees,
Nothing's undoing among the self-stung unfolding of things.

FROM

SCAR TISSUE

APPALACHIAN FAREWELL

Sunset in Appalachia, bituminous bulwark
Against the western skydrop.
An Advent of gold and green, an Easter of ashes.

If night is our last address,
This is the place we moved from,
Backs on fire, our futures hard-edged and sure to arrive.

These are the towns our lives abandoned,
Wind in our faces,
The idea of incident like a box beside us on the Trailways seat.

And where were we headed for?
The country of Narrative, that dark territory
Which spells out our stories in sentences, which gives them an end
                                        and beginning . . .

Goddess of Bad Roads and Inclement Weather, take down
Our names, remember us in the drip
And thaw of the wintry mix, remember us when the light cools.

Help us never to get above our raising, help us
To hold hard to what was there,
Orebank and Reedy Creek, Surgoinsville down the line.

LAST SUPPER

I seem to have come to the end of something, but don't know what,
Full moon blood orange just over the top of the redbud tree.
Maundy Thursday tomorrow,
                    Then Good Friday, then Easter in full drag,
Dogwood blossoms like little crosses
All down the street,
                    lilies and jonquils bowing their mitred heads.

Perhaps it's a sentimentality about such fey things,
But I don't think so. One knows
There is no end to the other world,
                    no matter where it is.
In the event, a reliquary evening for sure,
The bones in their tiny boxes, rosettes under glass.

Or maybe it's just the way the snow fell
                    a couple of days ago,
So white on the white snowdrops.
As our fathers were bold to tell us,
                    it's either eat or be eaten.
Spring in its starched bib,
Winter's cutlery in its hands. Cold grace. Slice and fork.

THE SILENT GENERATION II

We've told our story. We told it twice and took our lumps.
You'll find us here, of course, at the end of the last page,
Our signatures scratched in smoke.

Thunderstorms light us and roll on by.
Branches bend in the May wind,
But don't snap, the flowers bend and do snap, the grass gorps.

And then the unaltered gray,
Uncymbaled, undrumrolled, no notes to set the feet to music.
Still, we pull it up to our chins; it becomes our lives.

Garrulous, word-haunted, senescent,
Who knew we had so much to say, or tongue to say it?
The wind, I guess, who's heard it before, and crumples our pages.

And so we keep on, stiff lip, slack lip,
Hoping for words that are not impermanent—small words,
Out of the wind and the weather—that will not belie our names.

THE WRONG END OF THE RAINBOW

It must have been Ischia, Forio d'Ischia.
Or Rome. The Pensione Margutta. Or Naples
Somewhere, on some dark side street in 1959

With What's-Her-Name, dear golden-haired What's-Her-Name.
                                        Or Yes-Of-Course
In Florence, in back of S. Maria Novella,
And later wherever the carabinieri let us lurk.

Milano, with That's-The-One, two streets from the Bar Giamaica.
Venice and Come-On-Back,
                            three flights up,
Canal as black as an onyx, and twice as ground down.

Look, we were young then, and the world would sway to our sway.
We were riverrun, we were hawk's breath.
Heart's lid, we were center's heat at the center of things.

Remember us as we were, amigo,
And not as we are, stretched out at the wrong end of the rainbow,
Our feet in the clouds,
                        our heads in the small, still pulse-pause of age,

Gazing out of some window, still taking it all in,
Our arms around Memory,
Her full lips telling us just those things
                              she thinks we want to hear.

A FIELD GUIDE TO THE BIRDS

OF THE UPPER YAAK

A misty rain, no wind from the west,
Clouds close as smoke to the ground,
                    spring's fire, like a first love, now gone to ash,
The lives of angels beginning to end like porch lights turned off
From time zone to time zone,
                         our pictures still crooked on the walls,
Our prayer, like a Chinese emperor, always two lips away,
Our pockets gone dry and soft with lint.
Montana morning, a cold front ready to lay its ears back.

If I were a T'ang poet, someone would bid farewell
At this point, or pluck a lute string,
                              or knock on a hermit's door.
I'm not, and there's no one here.
The iconostasis of evergreens across the two creeks
Stands dark, unkissed and ungazed upon.
Tonight, it's true, the River of Heaven will cast its net of strung stars,
But that's just the usual stuff.
                    As I say, there's no one here.

In fact, there's almost never another soul around.
There are no secret lives up here,

                                    it turns out, everything goes
Its own way, its only way,
Out in the open, unexamined, unput upon.
The great blue heron unfolds like a pterodactyl
Over the upper pond,

                          two robins roust a magpie,
Snipe snipe, the swallows wheel, and nobody gives a damn.

A SHORT HISTORY OF MY LIFE

Unlike Lao Tzu, conceived of a shooting star, it is said,
And carried inside his mother's womb
For 62 years, and born, it's said once again, with white hair,
I was born on a Sunday morning,
                              untouched by the heavens,
Some hair, no teeth, the shadows of twilight in my heart,
And a long way from the way.
Shiloh, the Civil War battleground, was just next door,
The Tennessee River soft shift at my head and feet.
The dun-colored buffalo, the sands of the desert,
Gatekeeper and characters,
                              were dragon years from then.

Like Dionysus, I was born for a second time.
From the flesh of Italy's left thigh, I emerged one January
Into a different world.
                    It made a lot of sense,
Hidden away, as I had been, for almost a life.
And I entered it open-eyed, the wind in my ears,
The slake of honey and slow wine awake on my tongue.
Three years I stood in S. Zeno's doors,
                              and took, more Rome than Rome,
Whatever was offered me.

The snows of the Dolomites advanced to my footfalls.
The lemons of Lago di Garda fell to my hands.

Fast-forward some forty-five years,
                              and a third postpartum blue.
But where, as the poet asked, will you find it in history?
Alluding to something else.
Nowhere but here, my one and only, nowhere but here.
My ears and my sick senses seem pure with the sound of water.
I'm back, and it's lilac time,
The creeks running eastward unseen through the dank morning,
Beginning of June. No light on leaf,
No wind in the evergreens, no bow in the still-blond grasses.
The world in its dark grace.
                              I have tried to record it.

CONFESSIONS OF A

SONG AND DANCE MAN

The wind is my music, the west wind, and cold water
In constant motion.
                              I have an ear
For such things, and the sound of the goatsucker at night.
And the click of twenty-two cents in my pants pocket
That sets my feet to twitching,
                                        that clears space in my heart.

"We are nothing but footmen at the coach of language,
We open and close the door."
                              Hmmm two three, hmmm two three.
"Only the language is evergreen,
                                        everything else is seasonal."
A little time step, a little back-down on the sacred harp.
"Language has many mothers, but only one father."

                              ⸺

The dying *narcissus poeticus* by the cabin door,
Bear grass, like Dante's souls,
                              flame-flicked throughout the understory,
The background humdrum of mist

Like a Chinese chant and character among the trees,
Like dancers wherever the wind comes on and lifts them . . .

The stillness of what's missing
                            after the interwork's gone,
A passing sand step, a slow glide and hush to the wings—
A little landscape's a dangerous thing, it seems,
Giving illusion then taking it back,
                            a sleight of hand tune
On a pennywhistle, but holding the measure still, holding the time.

                         —

A God-fearing agnostic,
                            I tend to look in the corners of things,
Those out-of-the-way places,
The half-dark and half-hidden,
                            the passed-by and over-looked,
Whenever I want to be sure I can't find something.
I go out of my way to face them and pin them down.

Are you there, Lord, I whisper,
                            knowing he's not around,
Mumble *kyrie eleison*, mumble O three-in-none.
Distant thunder of organ keys
In the fitful, unoccupied
                            cathedral of memory.
Under my acolyte's robes, a slip-step and glide, slip-step and a glide.

—

Red-winged blackbird balancing back and forth on pond reed,
Back and forth then off then back again.
What is it he's after,
                              wing-hinge yellow and orange,
What is it he needs down there
In snipe country, marsh-muddled,
                              rinsed in long-day sunlight?

The same thing I need up here, I guess,
A place to ruffle and strut,
                              a place to perch and sing.
I sit by the west window, the morning building its ruins
In increments, systematically, across the day's day.

Make my bed and light the light,
                              I'll be home late tonight, blackbird, bye-bye.

COLLEGE DAYS

Mooresville, North Carolina, September 1953.
Hearts made of stone, doodly wop, doodly wop, will never break . . . I
Should have paid more attention, *doodly wop, doodly wop,*
To the words and not just the music.
Stonestreet's Café,
                    the beginning of what might be loosely called
My life of learning and post-adolescent heartbreak-without-borders.
All I remember now is four years of Pabst Blue Ribbon beer,
A novel or two, and the myth of Dylan Thomas—
American lay by, the academic chapel and parking lot.
O, yes, and my laundry number, 597.

What does it say about me that what I recall best
Is a laundry number—
                    that only reality endures?
Hardly. Still, it's lovely to hope so,
That speculation looms like an ever-approaching event
Darkly on the horizon,
                    and bids us take shelter,
Though, like Cavafy's barbarians, does not arrive.
That's wishful thinking, Miguel,
But proper, I guess,
                    to small rooms and early morning hours,

Where juke joints and clean clothes come in as a second best.
Is sin, as I said one time, more tactile than a tree?

Some things move in and dig down
                              whether you want them to or not.
Like pieces of small glass your body subsumes when you are young,
They exit transformed and easy-edged
Many years later, in middle age, when you least expect them,
And shine like Lot's redemption.
College is like this, a vast, exact,
                              window of stained glass
That shatters without sound as you pass,
Year after year disappearing, unnoticed and breaking off.
Gone, you think, when you are gone, thank God. But look again.
Already the glass is under your skin,
                              already the journey's on.

There is some sadness involved, but not much.
                              Nostalgia, too, but not much.
Those years are the landscape of their own occasions, nothing lost,
It turns out, the solemn sentences metabolized
Into the truths and tacky place mats
We lay out
         when custom demands it.
That world becomes its own image, for better or worse
—the raven caws, the Weed-Eater drones—

And has no objective correlative to muscle it down.
It floats in the aether of its own content,
                                    whose grass we lie on,
Listening to nothing. And to its pale half brother, the nothingness.

NIGHT THOUGHTS

UNDER A CHINA MOON

Out here, where the clouds pass without end,
One could walk in any direction till water cut the trail,
The Hunter Gracchus in his long body

                        approaching along the waves
Each time in his journey west of west.

BEDTIME STORY

The generator hums like a distant *Ding an sich*.
It's early evening, and time, like the dog it is,

is hungry for food,

And will be fed, don't doubt it, will be fed, my small one.
The forest begins to gather its silences in.
The meadow regroups and hunkers down

for its cleft feet.

Something is wringing the rag of sunlight

inexorably out and hanging.

Something is making the reeds bend and cover their heads.
Something is licking the shadows up,
And stringing the blank spaces along, filling them in.
Something is inching its way into our hearts,

scratching its blue nails against the wall there.

Should we let it in?

Should we greet it as it deserves,

Hands on our ears, mouths open?
Or should we bring it a chair to sit on, and offer it meat?
Should we turn on the radio,

should we clap our hands and dance

The Something Dance, the welcoming Something Dance?

I think we should, love, I think we should.

TRANSPARENCIES

Our lives, it seems, are a memory
                      we had once in another place.
Or are they its metaphor?
The trees, if trees they are, seem the same,
                        and the creeks do.
The sunlight blurts its lucidity in the same way,
And the clouds, if clouds they really are,
                       still follow us,
One after one, as they did in the old sky, in the old place.

I wanted the metaphor, if metaphor it is, to remain
                       always the same one.
I wanted the hills to be the same,
And the rivers too,
               especially the old rivers,
The French Broad and Little Pigeon, the Holston and Tennessee,
And me beside them, under the stopped clouds and stopped stars.
I wanted to walk in that metaphor,
                   untouched by time's corruption.

I wanted the memory adamantine, never-changing.
I wanted the memory amber,
            and me in it,

A figure among its translucent highlights and swirls,
Mid-stride in its glittery motions.
I wanted the memory cloud-sharp and river-sharp,
My place inside it transfiguring, ever-still,
                                        no wind and no wave.

But memory has no memory. Or metaphor.
It moves as it wants to move,
                            and never measures the distance.
People have died of thirst in crossing a memory.
Our lives are summer cotton, it seems,
                            and good for a season.
The wind blows, the rivers run, and waves come to a head.
Memory's logo is the abyss, and that's no metaphor.

MORNING OCCURRENCE AT XANADU

Swallows are flying grief-circles over their featherless young,
Night-dropped and dead on the wooden steps.
The aspen leaves have turned gray,
                                    slapped by the hard, west wind.

Someone who knows how little he knows
Is like the man who comes to a clearing in the forest,
                                    and sees the light spikes,
And suddenly senses how happy his life has been.

WRONG NOTES

To bring the night sky to life,

                       strike a wrong note from time to time,

Half for the listening ear, half for the watching eye.

Up here, just north of the Cabinet Mountains,

                             the Great Bear

Seems closer to me than the equinox, or rinsed glints

In the creek hurrying elsewhere into evening's undergrowth.

The same way with the landscape.

                         Our meadow, for instance,

Has two creeks that cross it;

                they join and become one about halfway down.

And that runs under my west window.

These are the flash and lapped scales

That trouble the late sunlight,

                  and spark the moon fires and moon dregs.

At other times, it seems invisible, or they do,

Moving slowly in dark slides

                    from beaver break to beaver break,

Muscling down from spruce shadow through willow shadow.

Above its margins the deer graze,

                    two coyotes skulk and jump,

And clouds start to herd together like wounded cattle.

And what does this matter?
                              Not much, unless you're one of those,
As I am, who hears a music in such things, who thinks,
When the sun goes down, or the stars do,
That the tune they're doing is his song,
That the instruments of the given world
                              play only for him.

THE MINOR ART OF SELF-DEFENSE

Landscape was never a subject matter, it was a technique,
A method of measure,
                        a scaffold for structuring.
I stole its silences, I stepped to its hue and cry.

Language was always the subject matter, the idea of God
The ghost that over my little world
Hovered, my mouthpiece for meaning,
                        my claw and bright beak . . .

SCAR TISSUE

What must be said can't be said,
It looks like; nobody has a clue,
                    not even, its seems, the landscape.
One hears it in dreams, they say,
Or out of the mouths of oracles, or out of the whirlwind.

I thought I heard it, a whisper, once,
In the foothills of the Dolomites,
                    night and a starless sky,
But who can remember, a black night, a starless sky,
Blurred voice and a blurred conceit.

It takes a crack in the membrane,
                    a tiny crack, a stain,
To let it come through; a breath, a breath like a stopped sigh
From the land of foreign tongues.
It is what it has to say, sad stain of our fathers.

                    —

Whatever is insignificant has its own strength,
Whatever is hidden, clear vision.
Thus the ant in its hide-and-seek,
                    thus the dung beetle,
And all the past weight of the world it packs on its back.

The insect world has no tongue to let loose, and no tongue to curb,
Though all day and all night it cries out.
Who says we shouldn't listen to them?
Who says we shouldn't behave ourselves as they do,

no noise but for one purpose?

Whatever the root sees in the dark is infinite.
Whatever the dead see is the same.
Listen, the rivers are emptying

under our feet,
Watched over by all the waters of the underworld.

———

Why does one never tire of looking out at the obvious?
The merely picturesque

is good for a day or so,
The ugly fascinates for a little while, then scabs over, like grease.
Only the obvious, with its odd neck, holds us close,

The endless sky with its endless cargo of cloud parts,
The wind in the woebegone of summer afternoons,
The landscape in its last lurch,
The shadowy overkill

of the evening sun going down.

It seems, somehow, to ignite us into a false love for the physical world.
Our mouths full of ashes, our mouths full of fresh fire,

phoenix-like,

Wide wings over wider lives,
We open and close on demand, we open and close.

—

The woods are thick with sunlight.
Tonight, over the mountain,
                              the full moon will replenish them
With their own reflected face.

—

This is the almost hour,
                              almost darkness, almost light,
Far northern dusk dust sifting over the evergreens,
Chiaroscuro at heaven's walk,
Charcoal and deeper shades where our foot falls and hands hang.

This is the time of mixed masks.
This is the time of sour songs,
                              of love gone wrong, of sixes and sevens,
The almost hour, the zero-zero.
This is the one place we feel at home, this is our zone.

The idea of horses grazes in deep, black grass.
The idea of separation
                              unleashes its luminous line
That holds us at either end.
How happy we are here, how utterly dark our contentment.

———

Friday, a little perch, a branch, to rest on for a moment.
Yesterday, Thursday,
I rose and fell like a firefly,
                    light off, light back on.
Today, I'm a hummingbird
On Friday's slick branch,
                    my heart like a beat machine, my wings a green itch.

———

It is impossible to say good-bye to the past.
Whose images are they anyway,
                    whose inability to spell them out?
Such destitution of words.
What hand was seen to wave in the all-absorbing light?

Better to leave it alone.
Better to let it drift there,
                    at the end edge of sight,
Replete with its angel bands and its handfuls of golden hair,
Just out of earshot, just out of reach.

But someday that hand will reappear
Out of the awful blear-light.
Someday that hand, white hand in the white light,
                    will wave again, and not stop.
No reason to look around then, it will be waving to you.

The slit wrists of sundown

                              tincture the western sky wall,

The drained body of daylight trumps the Ecclesiast

In its step down and wide walk,

Whose cloak is our salve and damp cloth,

                                    whose sigh is our medicine . . .

Chipmunk towering like a dinosaur

                                 out of the short grass,

Then up the tamarack, sparrow harrowing, then not,

Grasshopper in its thin, green armor,

Short hop, long bound, short hop and a long bound,

Life and death in the milky sunshine now,

                                    and concealing shade,

Sparrow avenging machine in the crush of inalterable law.

The arching, drought-dried pilot grasses,

                                 earwigged and light-headed,

Nod in the non-wind, directing the small ones nowhere.

Robin lands on the stump root,

Something red and just cut in its beak.

Chipmunk down from the tamarack,

                                and back on patrol,

In and out of the alleyways and sun spots of his saurian world.

———

The thread that dangles us

          between a dark and a darker dark,

Is luminous, sure, but smooth sided.

Don't touch it here, and don't touch it there.

          Don't touch it, in fact, anywhere—

Let it dangle and hold us hard, let it flash and swing.

———

The urge toward form is the urge toward God,

          perfection of either

Unhinged, unutterable.

Hot wind in the high country, an east wind, prairie wind.

Unutterable in cathedral or synagogue.

Unhinged, like low wind in high places.

Wind urge and word urge,

          last form and final thing, the O.

Great mouth. Toothless, untouched.

          Into whose night sky we all descend.

Star-like we list there

Restructured, forms within forms.

Meanwhile, the morning's sonogram

          reveals us just as we are,

Birds on their bright courses, the dogs at work in the field,

Flies at the windowpanes, and horses knee-deep in their deep sin.

Hard to forget those autumn evenings
                              driving out to the lake
To catch the sunset,
Harold's wallet already tucked and soft in my coat pocket,
Garda breaking aluminum-like
And curled as the dropping sun sponged out
                              villas and lemon trees,
Gardone shrinking into its own shadow as Friday night came down
Across the water,
Sirmio glittering like an olive leaf
                              turned upside down in the west wind,
Riva gone dark under sunset clouds,
The town of Garda itself
Below us with its fistful of lights beginning to come on,
Pulling us down like a centrifuge to the lake's edge,
Where we parked by the plane tree at the Taverna's door . . .
Those were the days, boys, those were the days.

The bulging blue of July
                              presses us down, and down,
Until the body of the world beneath us slurs to a halt,
Prelapsarian stillness at hand,
Something glistening in the trees,
                              angel wings starting to stir the dust,

The flatness of afternoon
Exacting, a sleep inside a sleep,
Our tongues like turnip greens,

                our dreams a rodeo dog's.

———

There is a dearth of spirit as weightless as the grave
That weighs and prefigures us.
It's like the smoke of forest fires from hundreds of miles away
That lies low in the mountains
And will not move,

           that holds us down with the tiredness of long afternoons,
So weightless the covering, so weightless the spread that spreads it.

There is a desperation for unknown things, a thirst
For endlessness that snakes through our bones
Like a lit fuse looking for Lethe,

                   whose waters reward us,
Their blackness a gossamer and grief
Lifted and laid to one side,
Whose mists are like smoke from forest fires that will not move.

———

Ravens are flying in and out of the summer woods.
Two, I think, no, three, each buzzed,

                 then buzzed again by a blackbird
Up from the tall reeds by the pond's edge.

The ravens bleat and the blackbirds attack and fall back,
Attack again, the ravens
Upstream by now, little dark points, the blackbirds invisible
As yesterday's prayers.
                    But working hard, Lord, working hard.

SCAR TISSUE II

Time, for us, is a straight line,
                         on which we hang our narratives.
For landscape, however, it all is a circling
From season to season, the snake's tail in the snake's mouth,
No line for a story line.
In its vast wheel, in its endless turning,
                                 no lives count, not one.

Hard to imagine that no one counts,
                          that only things endure.
Unlike the seasons, our shirts don't shed,
Whatever we see does not see us,
                          however hard we look,
The rain in its silver earrings against the oak trunks,
The rain in its second skin.

Pity the people, Lord, pity their going forth and their coming back,
Pity their sumptuous barricades
                         against the dark.
Show them the way the dirt works.
Show them its sift, the aftermath and the in-between.
Wet days are their own reward for now,
                         litter's lapse and the pebble's gleam.

Once in a while, we all succumb

                        to the merely personal,

Those glass shards and snipped metal

That glitter and disappear and glitter again

                                in the edged night light

Of memory's anxious sky.

How could it be otherwise, given our histories?

Like Dante's souls of the blessed,

                           they drop from their tiers

Down to our mind's eye

In whichever heaven it happens to be, for a few words,

An inch of adrenaline,

A slipped heartbeat or so,

                       before they begin to flicker and grain out.

Names, and the names of things, past places,

Lost loves and the love of loss,

The alphabet and geometry of guilt, regret

For things done and things undone,

All of the packaging and misaddresses of our soiled lives—

Ingrid under the archway on Via Giulia,

Quel ramo del Lago di Como,

                       Mt. Ann and the twice-thwarted tower,

Betsy, the White Rabbit, between the columns at Sweet Briar,
San Zeno sun strobe,
                    Goldstein and Thorp,
Flashes like bottle glass, no help for it, flashes like foxfire.

                            ▬▬▬

Spirit, subjective correlative and correspondent, moves
Like water under the skin of every story line,
Not too deep, but deep enough,
                            not too close to the top.

There are no words for these words,
Defining and erasing themselves without a sound
Simultaneously,
                    larger and smaller, puddle and drift.

In all superstition there lingers a heart of unbelief
For those who walk slipstitch upon the earth
                                and lose their footprints.
One signs one's name wherever it falls.

                            ▬▬▬

The wind never blows in the wrong place,
The sunrise is never late,
                    some Buddhist must certainly have said once.
If not, what a missed sound bite.
The natural world is always in step, and on time,

Absit omen our self-absorption.
Sometimes you eat the bear,

            and sometimes the bear eats you.

All morning, out of the sunlight, grainy subtraction,
I've courted the shadow life,
Asleep, or half-asleep,

            like a fish in a deep stream.
Dark spot, bright spot, leopard-skin water.
I feel it drifting around me,

            my life like a boat
Overhead, floating, unoccupied, back out of sight.

            ▬

I love to look at the new moon through the bare branches of
    winter trees.
Always the same moon, the same branches,
Always new entrances

            and caustic geographies.
The stars are still visible, like stunned impurities
In the great sea of anthracite that is the night sky.

One never gets used to this—
Immensity and its absolute,

            December chill
Like fingernails on the skin—

That something from far away has cracked you,

ever so slightly,

And entered and gone, one never should.

———

Virginia, Hanover County, December lastlight
Draining into a small hole
Behind the winter wickery

of hardwoods and cedar spires
That bordered three fields of soybean stobs
And uncut sumac runners and dead seed millet stalks.

My son and I and the kind man whose acres these were,
Shotgun and bird whirr,

day, and the drift of day, sun spill,
I've written it all down in footprints in rubbed red clay,
And put it aside, but find
It's no use, you can't keep anything you can't keep your hands on.

———

A small rain, a feathery, small rain,

has been falling all day
In the neighborhood.
Nothing comes clear, however, nothing is brought to bear.
It snoods our curls, it glosses our lips.
Garbage sacks gleam with a secret light.

Low overhead,

Just north of noon, the gray clouds keep on washing their hands
Obsessively, as though they had something still to prove.
1:51 p.m., and all's well
Elsewhere,
                    winter settling over the earth like a parachute
From nowhere, pulled open by no one you'd ever know.

—

Full moon like a 60-watt bulb across the backyard.
This is the light we live in.
This is the light the mind throws
                            against the dark, faint as a finger rub
On a rosary.
It doesn't care how old we are, or where our age will take us.
Nor does the darkness, friend,
                      whose love is a mystery.
Nor does what lies behind it, which isn't.

—

The outfit was out of town a couple of clicks,
                          on Via Mantovana,
A chain-link fence, a graveled car park,
Black Chevys, a deuce-and-a-half and a jeep or two
Under the blue Italian sky,
                all on the q.t.
The 430th CIC Detachment, your tax dollars at work.
Our job was to spy on our own troops and host country.

Great duty for a twenty-three-year-old, 1959,
The officers all about to retire after twenty years
Of service, the sergeants too,
Leaving the rest of us to put in our time,

                    two years or four,
Cruising the culture and its sidebars.
On down the road from our light cover,
Just north of Mantova one day after work, Ed DiCenzo and I
Sat in the sunset dripping into the plane trees
                    and Mincio River
Watching an eel fisherman through the trattoria window,
Both eating roast chicken and *tortellini con le gonne*,
The world in its purity and grace,
                    at least for a moment,
Giving our hearts a heads-up and a shoulder to lean on. Great duty.

                    ▬

Sunrise, a cold almost deep enough to crack the oaks,
Morning, like strawberry Kool-Aid,
                    spilling up from the Tidewater.
Middle of January, winter smooth-hipping down the runway.

Hillocks and patches of last week's snow
                    huddle and desiccate across the backyard,
Still white and vaguely funereal in the sweet light.
Squirrel tails flick like beavers', birds sing.

All day the wind will comb out its hair through the teeth of the
   evergreens.
All day the sunlight will sun itself
On the back porch of the cottage, out of the weather.

The world has an infinite beauty, but not, always, for us.
The stars will be boutonnieres,

                          though not necessarily for us.
And the grave is a resting place, but not, however, for one and all.

———

New skin over old wounds, colorless, numb.
Let the tongue retreat, let the heart be dumb.

APPALACHIA DOG

I can see it still, chopped and channeled, dual pipes,
Metallic red, *Appalachia Dog*
                              in black script on the left front door.
A major ride, dragging the gut in Kingsport in 1952.
A Ford, lowlife and low-down.
Up and back, then left at J. Fred's
                              and west out of town
Into legend and legend's underhalf, its twisted telling.

The rear end was dropped, as though the trunk was leaded for
    hauling.
Shine running, we said,
Pretending to know something about
                              something we knew nothing about,
Zeke Cleek and the Moose Lodge boys,
                              Junior Johnson's Grey Ghost
Mercury over in North Carolina, the Dog
Flickering in the downtown lights like a candle flame.

We never saw it again.
And over the years, when those days are lifted out
                              from their dark drawers,

The pegged pants with their welt seams, the Mr. B collars,
The Les Paul and Mary Ford 78s broken in half,
That '49 Ford is still there,
                    taillights like nobody's eyes,
Low-riding west toward the rising sun.

GET A JOB

Just over sixteen, a cigarette-smoking boy and a bit,
I spent the summer digging ditches,
And carrying heavy things
                    at Bloomingdale School site.
I learned how a backhoe works, and how to handle a shovel,
And multiple words not found in the dictionary.
Sullivan County, Tennessee, a buck twenty an hour,
1952.
      Worst job of my life, but I stuck it out.

Everyone else supported a family, not me.
I was the high school kid, and went home
Each night to my mother's cooking.
                    God knows where the others went.
Mostly across the line into Scott County, Virginia, I think,
Appalachian appendix, dead end.
Slackers and multipliers, now in, now out of jail, on whom I
    depended.
Cold grace for them.
           God rest them all road ever they offended,

To rhyme a prominent priest.
            Without a ministry, without portfolio,

Each morning I sought them out
For their first instructions, for their laying on of hands.
I wish I could say that summer changed my life,

$\qquad\qquad\qquad$ or changed theirs,

But it didn't. Apparently, nothing ever does.
I did, however, leave a skin there.
A bright one, I'm told, but less bright than its new brother.

ARCHAEOLOGY

The older we get, the deeper we dig into our childhoods,
Hoping to find the radiant cell
That washed us, and caused our lives
                                    to glow in the dark like clock hands
Endlessly turning toward the future,
Tomorrow, day after tomorrow, the day after that,
                                    all golden, all in good time.

Hiwassee Dam, North Carolina.
                                    Still 1942,
Still campfire smoke in both our eyes, my brother and I
Gaze far out at the lake in sunflame,
Expecting our father at any moment, like Charon, to appear
Back out of the light from the other side,
        low-gunwaled and loaded down with our slippery dreams.

Other incidents flicker like foxfire in the black
Isolate distance of memory,
                                    cross-eyed, horizon-haired.
Which one, is it one, is it any one that cleans us, clears us,
That relimbs our lives to a shining?

One month without rain, two months,
                                    third month of the new year,

Afternoon breeze-rustle dry in the dry needles of hemlock and pine.
I can't get down deep enough.
Sunlight flaps its enormous wings and lifts off from the backyard,
The wind rattles its raw throat,
                            but I still can't go deep enough.

HERACLITEAN BACKWASH

Wherever I am,
         I always wonder what I am doing back there,
Strange flesh in a stranger land.
As though the world were a window and I a faint reflection
Returning my gaze
Wherever I looked, and whatever I looked upon.

Absence of sunlight, white water among the tall trees.
Nothing whispers its secret.
Silence, for some, is a kind of healing, it's said,
         for others the end of a dark road
That begins the zone of a greater light.
Fish talk to the dead in the shallow water below the hill.

Or so the Egyptian thought,
         who knew a thing or two about such things.
Strange flesh in a stranger land.
The clouds take their toll.
Like moist souls, they litter the sky on their way to where they're not.
Dandelions scatter across the earth,
         fire points, small sunsqualls.

(FOR H.V., FIXED POINT IN THE FLUX)

CHINA TRACES

Nature contains no negatives.
                              Nothing is lost there,
The word is. Except the word.

In spring there is autumn in my heart,
My spirit, outside of nature, like slow mist in the trees,
Looking for somewhere to dissipate.

I write out my charms and spells
Against the passage of light
                              and gathering evil
Each morning. Each evening hands them back.

Out of the nothing nothing comes.
                              The rain keeps falling,
As we expected, the bitter and boundaryless rain.
The grass leaves no footprints,
                              the creek keeps on eating its one word.

In the night, the light assembles the stars
                              and tightens their sash.

MATINS

Sunlight like Vaseline in the trees,

                     smear and shine, smear and shine.
Ten days of rain and now the echoing forth of blank and blue
Through the evergreens.
Deer stand on their hind legs

                  in the bright meadow grasses.
The sound of the lilac upsurge rings bells for the bees.
Cloud puffs, like mortar rounds from the afterlife,

                          pockmark the sky.
Time, in its crystal goblet, laps and recedes, laps and recedes.

If we were the Rapture's child, if we
Were the Manichaean boy,
If we were the bodhisattva baby,

                today would be a good day
To let the light in, or send it out.
We're not, however. We're Nature's nobodies,

                   and we'd do well
To put on the *wu wei* slippers and find a hard spot
To sit on,

        sinking like nothing through the timed tides of ourselves.

NORTH

This is the north, cloud tatters trailing their joints across the ground
And snagging themselves
In the soaked boughs of the evergreens.
Even the heart could lift itself higher than they do,
The soaked and bough-spattered heart,
But doesn't because this is the north,
Where everything dark, desire and its extra inch, holds back
And drags itself, sullen and misty-mouthed, through the trees.
An apparitionless afternoon,
One part water, two parts whatever the light won't give us up.

The north is not the memory of the north but its repeat
And cadences, St. Augustine in blackface, and hand to mouth:
The north is where we go when there's no place left to go.
It's where our altered selves are,
Resplendent and unrepentant and wholly unrecognizable.
We've been here for years,
Fog-rags and rain and sun spurts,
Beforeworlds behind us, slow light spots like Jimmy Durante's
    fade-out
Hopscotching across the meadow grass.
This is our landscape and our landing zone, this is our dark glass.

IN PRAISE OF FRANZ KAFKA

Weather no matter, time no matter,
The immemorially long and windy body of the Hunter Gracchus
Floats again
Through the buoyant dark of the pine forest,
                                              ship-borne and laid out
Like a downed larch on the black, intransitive deckwork.
He passes each year
On the waters that circle above the earth
In his pitiless turn and endless geography.
The wings of the crewmen hang like washing along the railing.
June is his sunlight, and June is his farthering forth,
His world pure circumference.
                              Follow him if you can.

VESPERS

Who wouldn't wish to become
The fiery life of divine substance
                              blazing above the fields,
Shining above the waters,
The rain like dust through his fingerbones,
All our yearning like flames in his feathery footprints?
Who, indeed?
                    And still . . .

The world in its rags and ghostly raiment calls to us
With grinding and green gristle
Wherever we turn,
                    and we are its grist, and we are its groan.
Over the burned lightning strikes of tree shadows
                              branded across the near meadow,
Over the dusk-dazed heads of the oat grass,
The bullbat's chortle positions us, and holds us firm.

We are the children of the underlife,
                              at least for a time,
Flannel shirt on a peg, curled
Postcards from years past
                    thumbtacked along the window frames.

Outside, deer pause on the just-cut grass,
The generator echoes our spirit's humdrum,
                    and gnats drone high soprano . . .
Not much of a life, but I'll take it.

THE NARROW ROAD

TO THE DISTANT CITY

Heap me, Lord, heap me, we're heard to say,
Not really meaning it, but meaning
Gently, my man, ever so gently,
                              please lay me down,
Allow me all things I've not deserved,
Dandle my heart and tell me I'm still your baby boy.

How could it be otherwise,
                         our just meat being ash,
Which, don't worry, is set to be served at the next course.
We've said grace in the past tense.
We've said our prayers out of our mouths,
                                  not out of our hearts.
The more we talked, the more our tongues tied.

So pay us some nevermind.
Let us pretend the world's our own dream,
And be unto us as a hard wind
                         that understands nothing.
In fact, be yourself,
If that is what the nothing that is,
                    and the nothing that is to come, is called for.

PILGRIM'S PROGRESS

At the start, it goes like this—
One's childhood has a tremendous shape,

and moves like a wild animal

Through the deadfall and understory.
It's endlessly beautiful,

elusive and on to something.

It hides out, but never disappears.

Later, the sacred places Delphi and Italy on us,
Flicking and flashing through the forest,

half-seen, half-remembered.

And with them the woods itself,
Each tree, each interlude of marsh grass and beaver shade
Something to tug the sleeve with.

In the end, of course, one's a small dog
At night on the front porch,

barking into the darkness

At what he can't see, but smells, somehow, and is suspicious of.
Barking, poor thing, and barking,
With no one at home to call him in,

with no one to turn the light on.

GHOST DAYS

Labyrinthine, Byzantine,

                 memory's gold-ground mosaics

Still spill us and drop us short.

Who was the sixth guy in the Fiat 500

With Giancarlo, Pamela, the two drunken carabinieri and me

That New Year's Eve around 3 a.m.

Circling the Colosseum

               and circling the Colosseum?

And what year was it ten inches of snow descended

Like papal grace on Rome, and all the small *macchine*

Crashed on the Tiber's retaining wall?

                      What year was that?

The pieces clear and occlude like a retinal bleed.

And where are you now, Giancarlo,

               my first Italian friend,

Mad *marinaio* of the Via Margutta, where are you?

Like a black blot in a troubled eye,

                 you fall into place, then fall out

From the eyeball's golden dome.

How high you hung there once in our fast-faltering younger days.

How high we all hung,

             artificial objects in artificial skies,

Our little world like a little S. Apollinare in Classe,
Weedy and grass-gripped outside,
                                   white and glare-gold within,
Our saints with their wings missing,
But shining, nevertheless,
            as darkness gathers the darkness, and holds it tight.

THE SILENT GENERATION III

These are our voices, active, passive and suppressed,
                                 and these are our syllables.
We used them to love your daughters, we used them to love your
    sons.
We traveled, we stayed home, we counted our days out
                                 like prescription pills.
In the end, like everyone, we had too much to say.

                         ▬

We lived by the seat of our pants, we bet on the come
Only to come up short,
                         and see, as the smoke began to clear,
The life we once thought that boundless canopy of sky,
Was just the sound of an axe, echoing in the woods.

                         ▬

We hadn't the heart for heartlessness,
                         we hadn't the salt or the wound.
The words welled,
                 but goodness and mercy declined to follow us.
We carried our wings on our own backs, we ate our dead.
Like loose lightbulbs, we kept our radiance to ourselves.

                         ▬

Not heavy enough to be the hangman's burden,

                                        our noosed names

Are scrawled in the dust discursively, line after line.

Too strange for our contemporaries,

                              we'll prove to be

Not strange enough for posterity.

———

O you who come after us,

Read our remains,

                study the soundless bones and do otherwise.

TIME WILL TELL

Time was when time was not,
                          and the world an uncut lawn
Ready for sizing. We looked, and took the job in hand.
Birds burst from our fingers, cities appeared, and small towns
In the interim.
                 We loved them all.
In distant countries, tides nibbled our two feet on pebbly shores
With their soft teeth and languorous tongues.
Words formed and flew from our fingers.
                                 We listened and loved them all.

Now finitude looms like antimatter, not this and not that,
And everywhere, like a presence one bumps into,
Oblivious, unwittingly,
                        Excuse me, I beg your pardon.
But time has no pardon to beg, and no excuses.

The wind in the meadow grasses,
                             the wind through the rocks,
Bends and breaks whatever it touches.
It's never the same wind in the same spot, but it's still the wind,
And blows in its one direction,
                             northwest to southeast,

An ointment upon the skin, a little saliva,
Time with its murderous gums and pale, windowless throat,
Its mouth pressed to our mouths,
                    pushing the breath in, pulling it out.

HAWKSBANE

There are things that cannot be written about, journeys
That cannot be taken they are so sacred and long.

There is no nature in eternity, no wind shift, no weeds.

Whatever our vision, whatever our implement,
We looked in the wrong places, we looked for the wrong things.

We are not what is new, we are not what we have found.

THE WOODPECKER PECKS,

BUT THE HOLE DOES NOT APPEAR

It's hard to imagine how unremembered we all become,
How quickly all that we've done
Is unremembered and unforgiven,
                                how quickly
Bog lilies and yellow clover flashlight our footfalls,
How quickly and finally the landscape subsumes us,
And everything that we are becomes what we are not.

This is not new, the orange finch
And the yellow and dun finch
                                picking the dry clay politely,
The grasses asleep in their green slips
Before the noon can roust them,
The sweet oblivion of the everyday
                                like a warm waistcoat
Over the cold and endless body of memory.

Cloud-scarce Montana morning.
July, with its blue cheeks puffed out like a *putto* on an ancient map,
Huffing the wind down from the northwest corner of things,

Tweets on the evergreen stumps,

                        swallows treading the air,

The ravens hawking from tree to tree, *not you, not you,*

Is all that the world allows, and all one could wish for.

SINGING LESSON

This is the executioner's hour,
                             deep noon, hard light,
Everything edge and horizon-honed,
Windless and hushed, as though a weight were about to fall,
And shadows begin to slide from beneath things, released
In their cheap suits and eager to spread.

Out in the meadow, nothing breathes,
                             the deer seem to stop
Mid-jump at the fence, the swallows hanging like little hawks in
    the air.
The landscape loosens a bit, and softens.
                             Like miniature exhalations,
Wind stirs in the weeds, a dog barks, the shadows stretch and
    seep out.

Therefore, when the Great Mouth with its two tongues of water
    and ash
Shall say, Suffer the darkness,
Suffer the darkness to come unto you,
                           suffer its singsong,
And you will abide,
Listen to what the words spell, listen and sing the song.

LITTLEFOOT

1

It may not be written in any book, but it is written—
You can't go back,
                    you can't repeat the unrepeatable.
No matter how fast you drive, or how hard the slide show
Of memory flicks and releases,
It's always some other place,
                            some other car in the driveway,
Someone unrecognizable about to open the door.

Nevertheless, like clouds in their nebulous patterns,
We tend to recongregate
                    in the exitless blue
And try to relive our absences.
What else have we got to do,
The children reamplified in a foreign country,
The wife retired,
                  the farm like a nesting fowl and far away?

Whatever it was I had to say, I've said it.
Time to pull up the tie stakes.
I remember the way the mimosa tree
                         buttered the shade
Outside the basement bedroom, soaked in its yellow bristles.

I'll feed on that for a day or two.
I remember the way the hemlock hedge

burned in the side light.

Time to pull up the tie stakes.
Time to repoint the brickwork and leave it all to the weather.
Time to forget the lost eyelids,

the poison machine,
Time to retime the timer.
One's friends lie in nursing homes,

their bones broken, their hearts askew.
Time to retrench and retool.

We're not here a lot longer than we are here, for sure.
Unlike coal, for instance, or star clots.

Or so we think.
And thus it behooves us all to windrow affection, and spare,
And not be negligent.
So that our hearts end up like diamonds, and not roots.
So that our disregard evaporates

as a part of speech.

—

Cloud wisps, and wisps of clouds,

nine o'clock, a little mare's-tail sky
Which night chill sucks up.
Sundown. Pink hoofprints above the Blue Ridge,

soft hoofprints.

If this were the end of it, if this were the end of everything,
How easily one could fold
Into the lapping and overlapping of darkness.

                          And then the dark after that.

                —

Saturday's hard-boiled, easy to crack.

                    Sunday is otherwise,
Amorphous and water-plugged.
Sunday's the poem without people, all disappeared
Before the shutter is snapped.
Rainy vistas, wet-windowed boulevards, empty entrances.
Across the bridge, dissolute, one-armed,
Monday stares through the viewfinder,

                        a black hood over its head.

                —

When the rains blow, and the hurricane flies,

                      nobody has the right box
To fit the arisen in.
Out of the sopped earth, out of dank bones,
They seep in their watery strings

                    wherever the water goes.
Who knows when their wings will dry out, who knows their next
   knot?

                —

In the affinity is the affection,
                              in the affection everything else
That matters, wind in the trees,
The silence above the wind, cloud-flat October sky,
And the silence above that.

The leaves of the maple tree,
                              scattered like Post-it notes
Across the lawn with messages we'll never understand,
Burn in their inarticulation,
As we in ours,
              red fire, yellow fire.

It's all music, the master said, being much more than half right,
The disappearance of things
Adding the balance,
                    dark serenity of acceptance
Moving as water moves, inside itself and outside itself.

Compassion and cold comfort—
                              take one and let the other lie,
Remembering how the currents of the Adige
Shattered in sunlight,
Translucent on the near side,
                              spun gold on the other.

▬

Which heaven's the higher,

                       the one down here or the one up there?

Which blue is a bluer blue?

Bereft of meaning, the moon should know,

                         the silent, gossip-reflecting full moon.

But she doesn't, and no one descends to speak for her.

Time in its two worlds. No choice.

2

I am the sign, I am the letter.
I am the language that cannot be come to terms with.
I will go to my resting place
                                and will not be born again.
I am what is scattered and cannot be gathered up.
I am small, I am silence,
                                I am what is not found.

Moon like a hard drive
                        just over the understory
Freckling my neighbor's backyard,
Nightscreen unscrolling along the River of Heaven,
Celestial shorthand
Unasked for and undeletable
In time-lapse upon the early November skybook.

These are our last instructions,
                            of which we understand nothing.
The road map is there, the password,
                            neither of which we understand.
They boil on our tongues like waterflies.
They cling to our fingers,
                        they settle along our still eyelids
As though we would succor them,
As though we could understand their wing-buzz and small teeth.

—

Wherever I've gone, the Holston River has stayed next to me,
Like a dream escaping
                    some time-flattened orifice
Once open in childhood, migrating now like a road

I've walked on unknowingly,
                            pink and oblivious,
Attended by fish and paving stones,
The bottom breaks like mountains it slithers out of, tongued and
    chilled.

The river is negative time,
                            always undoing itself,
Always behind where it once had been.
Memory's like that,
Current too deep, current too shallow,
Erasing and reinventing itself while the world
Stands still beside it just so,
                            not too short, not too tall.

There's no uncertainty about it, negative time,
No numbering.
    Like wind when it stops, like clouds that are here then not here,
It is the pure presence of absence.
November's last leaves fall down to it,
The angels, their wings remodeled beneath their raincoats,
Live in it,
        our lives repeat it, skipped heartbeats, clocks with one hand.

Out of the sallows and slick traces of Southwest Virginia,
From Saltville and Gate City, from Church Hill and New Hope,

The river remainders itself
                    and rises again
Out of its own depletion.
How little we know it, how little we really remember it.
How like our own blood it powers on,
                              out of sight, out of mind.

                    ⸻

Outside of the church, no salvation,
St. Cyprian says.
Outside of nature, no transformation, I say,
                              no hope of return.
Like us, November doesn't know this,
Leaf ends curled up like untanned leather,
                    grass edges bleared back from emerald ease,
Light-loss diaphanous in the bare-backed and blitherless trees.

4

Well, the wings of time pass, the black wings,
And the light is not adumbrated,
                              or dampened down—
Like splendor, there is no end to it
Inside the imagination,
                    then inside of that,
Wind-beat, light of light, and even into the darkness.

5

November noon mist, gold coins of leaves
Glittering through it as though refracted by sunlight
Through rain shower,
                    radiant clusters, radiant change,

Mountains rehollowed and blotted out,
Car lights continuous rosary beads
                              both ways on the Interstate,
Evening already released out over the dark Atlantic.

These are the still days,
                    stillness being the metaphor
Out of which every grain is revealed
                              and is identified.
Finger me, Lord, and separate me to what I am.

                    ▬▬▬

In nature there is no past or future,
                              no pronouns, no verbs.
Old knowledge, Slick, old deadlights.
Still, the tongue does not know this, the half-lit and dumb tongue—

Precision of frogs and grasses,
                    precision of words,

Each singular, each distinct,
The tongue tries to freeze-frame them as they are,
                                    and offer them to us.

Now is precise but undefinable,
                        now is nonverbal,
No matter how hard we work it out.
Nuthatch or *narwhal*,
                    like petals, words drift in the air.

——

Calamities covet us, wild grass will cover our bodies,
We read in the Book of Poverty.
Deliver us, blessed immaculata,
                        adorn our affections.

Language is luckless and limitless,
                        as nature is.
But nature is not sincere, nor is it insincere—
The language of landscape is mute and immaculate.

First character of the celestial alphabet, the full moon,
Is a period, and that is that.
No language above to aid us,
                    no word to the wise.

——

I leave a blank for what I don't know,
                           four syllables, _____,
And what I will never know.
Thrones, and assisting angels, this is a comforting.

In Kingsport, looking across the valley toward Moccasin Gap
From Chestnut Ridge,
                        the winter-waxed trees
Are twiggy and long-fingery, fretting the woods-wind,

Whose songs, ghost songs, wind-lyrics from sixty years ago,
Float back and exhale—
                        I will twine with my mingles of raven black hair.
Will you miss me when I'm gone?

6

The winter leaves crumble between my hands,
                                    December leaves.
How is it we can't accept this, that all trees were holy once,
That all light is altar light,
And floods us, day by day, and bids us, the air sheet lightning
    around us,
To sit still and say nothing,
                        here under the latches of Paradise?

Sunset, line like a long tongue-lick above the Blue Ridge,
Mock orange, then tangerine, then blush.

                     How ordinary, dog,
The rush-hour car lights down Locust Avenue like quartz crystals,
Backlit and foraging forth.
Streetlights gather the darkness to them,
Compassion an afterthought,

                        mercy no thought at all.

Moon down, darkness fixed and unmoving,
Stars bobbing like water lights,

                       three weeks to the winter solstice,
Wind drift and tack from the north,
Night like a distance one could row on,
Whose depths are an afterlife

                   almost, whose sea is remembered
As half-crossed, its wave spray like wind-dust.

Good luck bamboo in three shoots in high-glaze south German
    brown vase,
Front yard like a windowpane
Into the anteroom of all things untouchable,

Cycladic ghost mask,
                    little Egyptian and Zuni overseers,
Choctaw and pre-Columbian artifacts arranged
Against the ruinous dark waters
                         outside the horizon.

———

Time is your mother in a blue dress.

———

When was it I first heard of the blank,
The salve of nothingness,
                    all its engendering attitude?
When was it I felt the liquid of absolution
And all its attendant emptiness
For the first time, and what it might mean?
Not young, I'd have to say,
                remembering not one thing about either of them.

How early, however, I learned of their opposites.
Muscadines plump in their plenitude,
Lake waters lowing at night under frog call,
                      night wind in leaf-locked trees,
Splash of the fishing lure, whisper of paddle blade and canoe,
Clouds like slow-moving cattle
Across the tiny and synchronized tip of the moon.

To walk up the Y-shaped hill

                         from the commissary

(This was a government town)

In summer under the hardwoods and conifers

Was to know the extension of things,

                         the deep weight of the endlessness

Of childhood, deep, invisible weight,

Lake-sound and lake-song in high hum, the future in links and
    chains.

To lie under lake-wind in August,

                         under mountain laurel

And blue-green North Carolina sky,

Lunch over, campfire smoke-ends

                         drifting out over water glints,

Was something like nothingness, perhaps, and its caress,

Crusader knights in their white tunics

                         and red crosses

Like ghosts through the trees, but not enough.

                        —

Precious memories, how they linger,

                         how they ever flood my soul,

In the stillness of the midnight,

                         precious, sacred scenes unfold.

8

Good luck is a locked door,

                    but the key's around somewhere.
Meanwhile, half-hidden under the thick staircase of memory,
One hears the footsteps go up and the footsteps go down.

As water mirrors the moon, the earth mirrors heaven,
Where things without shadows have shadows.
A lifetime isn't too much to pay

                    for such a reflection.

Three years, the story goes, it took the great ship to appear
In silhouette from the shadows
                              hanging above Lake Garda
And dock at the small port of Riva,
The Hunter Gracchus carried upon a bier by two men
In black tunics with silver buttons
Up to a back room in the mayor's office
                                   until it was time to return onboard

And circle the waters of the world.
Unable to set down on land,
                              unable to leave this world,
The story goes on, because of a wrong turn of the tiller
This side of the other shore,
Some inattention,
The great ship and the great body,
                              like lost love, languish and lip the earth,

Received sporadically, recognized everywhere,
The ship with its infinitely high masts,
                                   its sails in dark folds,
Cobalt and undulant rocking of lake swells and waves,
Long runners and smooth slatch of the seas,

Creek hiss and pond sway,
Landfall and landrise
                    like Compostela at land's end.

There is no end to longing.
There is no end to what touch sustains us,
                              winter woods
Deep in their brown study and torqued limbs,
Fish-scale gray of January sky,
Absence of saints on Sunday morning streets,
                                   the dark ship,
Dead leaves on the water, the muddy Rivanna and its muddy sides.

                    ▬

We all owe everything to those who preceded us,
Who, by the lightness of their footsteps,
Tap-danced our stories out, our techniques,
                              who allowed us to say
Whatever it was we had to say.
God rest them all in their long robes and vanishing shoes.
God grant that our figures be elegant,
                         our footwork worthy.

                    ▬

Faith is a thing unfathomable,
Though it lisp at our fingertips,
                    though it wash our hands.

There is no body like the body of light,

                                         but who will attain it?

Not us in our body bags,

Dark over dark, not us,

                  though love move the stars and set them to one side.

Sunlight like I beams through S. Zeno's west-facing doors,

As though one could walk there,

                          and up to the terraces

And gold lawns of the Queen of Heaven.

I remember the lake outside of town where the sun was going down.

I remember the figures on the doors,

                            and the nails that held them there.

The needle, though it has clothed many, remains naked,

The proverb goes.

                    So with the spirit,

Silver as is the air silver, color of sunlight.

And stitches outside the body a garment of mist,

Tensile, invisible, unmovable, unceasing.

The Holston, past Rotherwood,

                     clear white and powder white,

The hills dark jade and light jade,

All of it flowing southwest

                 against the wind and the wind noise,

Summer enfrescoed in stop-time

                   alongside the Cumberlands,

Leo and Virgo slow as a cylinder turn overhead,

Wind in the trees, wind on the water.

Like clouds, once gone in their long drift,

> there's no coming back—

And like the wind that moves them, we stop
Wherever we please, or wherever we come to be,
Each one in his proper place,

> not too near, not too far

From *That's okay* and *No one was ever interested enough.*

How many years have slipped through our hands?
At least as many as all the constellations we still can identify.
The quarter moon, like a light skiff,

> floats out of the mist-remnants

Of last night's hard rain.
It, too, will slip through our fingers

> with no ripple, without us in it.

How is it it's taken me almost a lifetime to come to the fact
That heaven and earth have no favorites

> in either extreme?

Bits of us set out, at one time or another, in both directions,
Sleeping fitfully, heads on our fists,
Now close together and warm, now cold in the south sky.

Each one arrives in his own fashion,

                           each one with his birthmark

Beginning to take shape and shine out

And lead forth like a lead lamp.

Look for us in the black spaces, somewhere in the outer dark.

Look for us under the dead grass

                    in winter, elsewhere, self-satisfied, apart.

A good writer is like a wind over meadow grass.

He bends the words to his will,

But is invisible everywhere.

Lament is strong in the bare places.

Among the winter trees, his words are fixed to music.

Or so we flatter ourselves,

                        sunset cloud tufts briquettes

Going ash in the ash-going sky.

We never look hard enough.

The grasses go back and forth, up and down, for thousands of miles,

But we don't look hard enough.

Every other building a church,

Each side of the road,

                    Orebank half a mile long

Under the hill until the last curve

Down to the highway, left to Kingsport, right to Bristol,
East toward the rising sun, west toward home.

"Through the years of dust and sand," Tao Chi lamented,
Meaning his worldly ambitions
                              —his "single unworthy thought"
That set him adrift on the floating world—
                                   his old age
Just recompense for what was not found,
Awaiting the great wash, a "final crash of thunder."

For half a lifetime, and more,
                              his days were the days of an ant,
His life, he thought, no longer than that of an insect
Going north on land,
                      going south on the raw rivers,
His last painting a single narcissus plant, his thoughts,
He wrote down, still wandering "beyond the boundless shores."

Water, apparently, is incomprehensible
At its beginning and at its end,

                        nothing into nothing,
And in between it's unsizable.
Certainly childhood water's that way,
The rivers coming from nowhere and going nowhere,
The lakes with no stopping place.
The waters of childhood are unimaginable.
The French Broad and Little Pigeon Rivers, the Holston,
Hiwassee and Cherokee Lakes,

                        Pickwick and Indian Path.
Water's immeasurable.

The heart is immeasurable,

                  and memory too.
Such little boxes to keep them in.
Like blue herons in heaven's field, they lift their long legs
Silently, and very slow,
In the ponds and back eddies they stalk through and rise from,
Air-colored in the sky-colored air.
How like the two of them to resettle then,

                        one hunting, one perched above.

Memory is a lonely observer,
                    the heart has thin legs.
They live in an infinite otherness, on dark snags,
In waters the color that they are,
                    and air is, the hard, endless air.

—

Snow, then sleet over snow, then snow again,
                          the footprints still firm
Into the dark beyond the light's fall.
Whiter inside the darkness to the south than the north.

Whatever has been will be again
                    in the mind, in the world's flow,
Invisible armies outside the windows in rank,
Footprints continuing into the vestibules of the end.

—

The light that shines forth from the emptiness does not sink,
They'd have you believe.
               As well as whatever is next to it,
They'd also have you believe.
Philosopher, they are not able, philosopher.
And her begot him, think that.

—

It's Groundhog Day, and sunlight is everywhere. Thank God.
Winter is such a comforting

                with its sleet and icy dreams.
Shadows abound, and raw twigs,
The sharp edge of the absolute still snug in its loamy bed,
The template of its wings like shadows across the grass.

What poverty the heat of noon is,
And how we embrace it hard in our dutiful duds.
Short February.
How we will miss you and the actual world,

                        the singular,
The frozen composition that pentimentos our sorrow.

Still, for the time being, we have the sunlight that eats away
At our joy,

        and still give thanks for that.
We try to count up the buttons on its golden coat,
But our eyes are unworthy.
We offer both our hands,

           but they are unworthy too.

And so we remain transfixed

              —the flowers from Delos
Unpurpled and stiff in their tarnished and silver bowl—
By sunlight,

Hoping the darkness will clear things up,
Hoping that what its handkerchief uncovers is what we get.

—

Just east of midnight,
                    the north sky scrolls from right to left,
A dark player piano.
No stopping the music, east to west,
                              no stopping it.

The small lights wander among the vacant trees like ghosts,
Whose roots have no voice in their deep sleep,
These lights that have no warmth in their drugged walk,
damp flames and feckless.

The stars drift like cold fires through the watery roots of heaven,
These stars that are floating plants.
The small lights are not like that,
but once were, I guess, light as a shadow.

What bodies will gather the lights in,
or the stars in?
What waters will float their anxious rest?
Altar of darkness, altar of light, which tide will take them in?

The great mouth of the west hangs open,
                        mountain incisors beginning to bite
Into the pink flesh of the sundown.
The end of another day
                in this floating dream of a life.
Renown is a mouthful, here and there.

Rivers and mountains glide through my blood.
Cold pillow, bittersweet years.
In the near distance, a plane's drone
                     rattles the windows.
Clear night. Wind like a predator
                  in the sharp grass of the past.

I find it much simpler now to see
                  the other side of my own death.
It wasn't always that way,
When the rivers were rivers and mountains were mountains.
Now, when the mouth closes,
               the wind goes out of everything.

—

Fame for a hundred years

                      is merely an afterlife,

And no friend of ours.

Better to watch the rain fall in the branches of winter trees.

Better to have your mail sent

To someone else in another town,

                        where frost is whiter than moonlight.

Horses, black horses:

                    Midnight, Five Minutes to Midnight.

Rider up, the sparks from their hooves like stars, like spiked stars.

This is a metaphor for failure,

This is the Rest of It, the beautiful horse, black horse.

Midnight. Dark horse, dark rider.

                      —

I love the lethargy of the single cloud,

                      the stillness of the sky

On winter afternoons, late on winter afternoons,

A little fan of light on the tips of the white pines.

I love the winter light, so thin, so unbuttery,

Transparent as plastic wrap

Clinging so effortlessly

                  to whatever it skins over.

—The language of nature, we know, is mathematics.
The language of landscape is language,
Metaphor, metaphor, metaphor,

                all down the line.

The sweet-breath baby light of a winter afternoon,
Boy-light, half-covered in blue,

                almost invisible as breath,
So still in the flower beds, so pale.

Four days till the full moon,

              light like a new skin on the dark
Quarter, like light unborrowed, hard,

                black hole with its golden floor.

Who knows the happiness of fish,

              their wind-raising, ordinary subtleties?
Describing the indescribable,
Image into idea,

          the transmission of the spirit,
It cannot be done.

The Chinese principle, *breath-resonance-life-motion*,
Engenders, it was believed.

As does the bone method of brushwork,
Creating structure

in poems as well as pictures.

Plotting in paint, place in poetry,
Completes composition,

the bedrock of spiritual values.
Competent, *marvelous*, and *divine*
Were the three degrees of accomplishment.

And still, it cannot be done.

Image resists all transmutation.
All art is meta-art, and has its own satisfactions.
But it's not divine,

as image is,
Untouchable, untransmutable,

wholly magic.

━━

Midnight Special, turn your ever-loving light on me.

1 5

You still love the ones you loved

                        back when you loved them—books,
Records, and people.
Nothing much changes in the glittering rooms of the heart,
Only the dark spaces half-reclaimed.

                              And then not much,
An image, a line. Sometimes a song.

Car doors slam, and slam again, next door.
Snow nibbles away at the edges of the dark ground.
The sudden memory of fur coats,

                         erotic and pungent,
On college girls in the backseats of cars, at Christmas,
Bourgeois America, the middle 1950s,

                             Appalachia downtown.

And where were we going? Nowhere.
Someone's house, the club, a movie?

                         See the pyramids along the Nile,
WKPT, *I'm itching like a man on a fuzzy tree.*
It didn't matter.
Martin Karant was spinning them out,

                        and the fur was so soft.

March is our master, the louche month we cannot control.
It passes like a river over us
—Cold current, warm spot—
                whose destination is always downstream,
Out of sight.
White water, easy water,
              March is a river over us.

Snow slam and sun burst,
              dead grass like peroxided hair
Unkempt among scattershot.
In Knoxville, across the street from James Agee's ex-house,
A small tree in full blossom,
Everything else still underground,
              river dark overhead.

I used to live here myself
            some sixty-five years ago.
Not here, precisely, but in the town,
Across town,
In a small house off the Kingston Pike,
No blossoming fruit limbs, no stripped, deciduous trees.

Love of the lack of love is still love

                         wherever you find it,

I once heard an old man say,

In March, when the wind was westerly

                     and the white clouds white as petals.

In March, in a vacant lot

On Chambliss Avenue, off the Kingston Pike.

                              And he was right.

———

I think I'm going to take my time,

                        life is too short

For immortality and its attendant disregards.

I have enough memories now for any weather,

Either here or there.

                I'll take my time.

Tomorrow's not what I'm looking forward to, or the next day.

My home isn't here, but I doubt that it's there either—

Empty and full have the same glass,

               though neither shows you the way.

———

Born again by water into the life of the spirit,

                   but not into the Life,

Rivers and lakes were my bread and wine,

Creeks were my transubstantiation.

              And everything's holy by now,

Vole crawl and raven flyby,
All of the little incidents that sprinkle across the earth.

Easy enough to say,
                      but hard to live by and palliate.
Camus said that life is the search for the way back
To the few great simple truths
We knew at the beginning.
Out of the water, out to the cold air, that seems about right.

—

The moon, over Susan's house,
                    gobba a ponente,
Heading west toward the western reaches.
Snow-strikes streak my hair.
                    We are all leaves in the current.

Leaning on Jesus, leaning on Jesus,

                              leaning on the everlasting love.

That's a tough lean, Hernando,

When all the hackles of spring are raised,

                          and its teeth glint

Like flint points in the sunshine,

Bright snarls from the underground.

Not much to lean on wherever you look,

                        above or below.

I remember my father in the spring,

                        who leaned on no one

And nothing, inspecting the rose plants

And the crusty, winter-warped mulch beds,

The blue distances over his back, over Cumberland Gap,

Opening like a great eye,

Jesus, he'd always say, Jesus, it's gone and done it again.

In Giorgio Morandi's bedroom and studio, it was always spring.

He would say, "Each time we begin,

                        we think we have understood,

That we have all the answers.

But it turns out we're just starting over again from the beginning."

Some bottles, a bed, and three tables,
The flowers abounding in little rectangles
                                        all over the walls.

                    ▬

Meanwhile, in New York City,
Branch limbs scrubbed bare by winter;
                                tiny fuses bumped at each end
Wait for Persephone's match.

                    ▬

Spring freeze, and tulips cover their heads
                                with iridescent hands;
Robins head for the hedges.
Even the insects back down
And cower inside their hiding holes.
Only the leaves seem cool, the new leaves,
Just butting their arrowed heads into the unforgiving blue.
How many lives these little ones lead.
                            I wish that one of them were mine.

                    ▬

A recluse should avoid the absolute,
                            and its hills.
Master of Words, Lord of Signs, you've left me, where are you?
Down by the muddy waters, feeding the brilliant birds?
Half-returned, half still going away?

Now that you've gone,
          I remember we've had an appointment there for years.
Don't move, I'm on my way.

It's quiet, no words, no words.
Is this just a silence, or just the start of the end?
Show yourself, Lord,
          Master of What Is About to Be.
Stars turn brown in the river.
We share no happiness here—
Step out of the Out,
          uncover your tongue and give me the protocol.

━━━

I'm starting to feel like an old man
          alone in a small boat
In a snowfall of blossoms,
Only the south wind for company,
Drifting downriver, the beautiful costumes of spring
Approaching me down the runway
          of all I've ever wished for.

Voices from long ago floating across the water.
How to account for
          my single obsession about the past?
How to account for
          these blossoms as white as an autumn frost?

Dust of the future baptizing our faithless foreheads.
Alone in a small boat, released in a snowfall of blossoms.

———

Don't forget me little darling when they lay me down to die.
Just this one wish little darling that I pray.
As you linger there in sadness you are thinking of the past,
Let your teardrops kiss the flowers on my grave.

It's been, say, five years since I've been back here at this hour,
Evening starting its light-curling plane

                      under the clouds,
The east-shrugged, flamingo clouds,
Everything different now, and everything just the same.
Except the leaves and birds,

                great-grandchildren, and great-great.

It's not tomorrow I'm looking forward to, it's yesterday,
Or, better yet, the day before that.
The wind keeps gossiping in both my ears for nothing.
I can't go back there,
No matter how juicy the stories are,

                no matter how true, or untrue.

We don't know much, really, but we do know some things.
We know the people we learned from,

                and know what we learned.
We have to be humble about that—
I know what I got, and I know where I got it from,
Their names inscribed in my Book of Light.

All the while we thought we were writing for the angels,
And find, after all these years,

Our lines were written in black ink on the midnight sky,
Messages for the wind,
                              a flutter of billets-doux
From one dark heart to the next.

———

Who knew it would take so many years to realize
—Seventy years—that everything's light—
The day in its disappearing, the night sky in its distance, false dawn,
The waters that rise beneath the earth,
Bat wings and shadow pools,
                              that all things come from splendor?

The cardinal in his fiery caul,
The year's first dandelion globe,
                              ash-gray on the ash-green lawn,
Dear tulip leaves, color of carp bellies, wisteria drools
Withered and drained dry—
All light in the gathering darkness,
                              a brilliance itself which is set to come.

———

The cloud poets of ancient China
Saw what they saw and recorded it,
                              diviners of what wasn't there,
Prestidigitators of nothingness.
                    Let me be one of them.

Sun over plum-colored leaf planes,

> shadows at ease in the east-going ivy.

A little wind, like a falling wind,

Tickles the planes, and they rise and fall.

Mid-May in the city garden,

> sunlight in designated spaces

Among the buildings, golden for us, dun-dust next door,

The sun like the Green Knight's head,

Rolling in slow motion toward its distant and dark corner,

Bright drops on the bright green hedge,

> black on the black borders.

In an opposite corner, splotches of sun and shade,

Like birthmarks all of us have,

Some on our faces, some on our hearts,

> all of them afterprints of our ruin,

Through which we step each morning

Gingerly, some of us going east, some of us going west.

This is the bird hour, peony blossoms falling bigger than wren hearts
On the cutting border's railroad ties,
Sparrows and other feathery things
Homing from one hedge to the next,

                             late May, gnat-floating evening.

Is love stronger than unlove?

                       Only the unloved know.
And the mockingbird, whose heart is cloned and colorless.

And who's this tiny chirper,

                      lost in the loose leaves of the weeping cherry tree?
His song is not more than three feet off the ground, and singular,
And going nowhere.
Listen. It sounds a lot like you, hermano.

                            It sounds like me.

Don't sew the skins of land and sea animals

                                into the same garment.

Over each grave, build a wooden house.

Burn children's toys to bring good weather.

And so on, the legends say.

                      Herons in mid-June stand up to their knees

In creek water, their wings like vinyl siding against their sides.

Next month they'll do the same thing.

Outside the cycle of seasons,

                         our lives appear meaningless,

No lilacs, no horse in the field, no heart-hurt, no sleeve:

Where time is constant and circular, all ends must meet.

                         ━

White clouds now dissipating in evening's turnaround,

No sound but the sound of no sound,

                         late sunlight falling on grass.

                         ━

A little knowledge of landscape whets isolation.

This is a country of water,

                      of water and rigid trees

That flank it and fall beneath its weight.
They lie like stricken ministers, gray and unredeemed.
The weight of water's unbearable,

and passes no judgment.
Side by side they lie, in intricate separation.

This is a country of deep inclemency, of strict
Self-immolation and strict return.
This is the way of the absolute,

dead grass and waste
Of water, clouds where it all begins, clouds where it ends,
Candle-point upshoots on all the upstart evergreens,
Sun behind west ridge,

no moon to sickle and shine through.

—

Much is unknown up here,

much more still left to be unexplained.
Under the pines there's not much to see,
White clouds and gray clouds,
The shadows they carry inside themselves unto the world's end.
That sort of business. It's hard.

There are fourteen cliff swallow round-mouthed mud nests

under the roof
Of the old barn house.
I stand and watch birds flying frantically after the rain,

Gold-breasted in the suddenly appearing sunlight.
Out of each hole a beak's unlevered.

Wang Wei had something to say about the unknowing:
Unable to throw off my remnant habits
I find the world has come to know me for them
My name and style—these they have right
But this heart of mine they still do not know.

Morning, a small rain on the cabin,
                              cloud tears like blown fire smoke
Under the slow overcast.
Nothing to do but watch the larch boughs,
Color, almost, of my shirt,
                        flourish their crystal studs.

What is the span of one's life?
How do you measure it
                    before it goes back to formlessness?
This is of some note to the white-haired.
Cubits or years, missed opportunities,
                        the minor, self-satisfied
Successes that came, as all things must, down to nothing,
The time it took to get there?

There is a resignation in all things deep as dirt,
A knowledge that no one lacks,
A force that finds its way
                              to the tip of every thing.
There is a serenity
Under our layers that rocks like a cradle of calm waters.
There is a freshness that we abide.

Deer huddle like cattle around the salt block,
                              then burst like flames in the air.
The white clouds slide from the south
Like an edge of ice.
The swallows harangue and arabesque
Over the lawn and lilac rim of the late lilacs,
Then dwindle against the dark green of the evergreens.

Last bird call, sun disappearing
                              under the right edge of things.
All that I know goes with it,
Isolate, like a body pulled down by weights
                              into the depths.

At seventy, it's always evening,

                light diluted,

Breeze like a limp hand

Just stirring the long-haired grasses, then letting them be.

The dark decade, beginning its long descent

                       out over the blank Atlantic,

Against the wind, inexorable,

The light dissolving like distance in the evergreens.

Even the clouds find a place to rest.

And that's the way it should be,

Swallows swarming like gnats

                in the gnat-infested air,

Tree shadows lying like limbed logs across the meadow,

Slowly sinking into the hill's shadow that stalks them.

Deer raise their white flags and leave the field,

The sapsucker leaves her nest

In the barn house wall,

        and everything moves toward its self-appointed end.

                  ———

I keep on thinking,

        If I sit here for long enough,

A line, one true line,
Will rise like some miraculous fish to the surface,
Brilliant and lithe in the late sunlight,
And offer itself into my hands.
I keep thinking that as the weeks go by,
                                    and the waters never change.
I keep thinking that as the sun goes down and the birds fly home.

The sky is cloudless, the meadow seems like a vast plain
Without dust,
                the Chinese vocabulary of the grasses
Shining like water wherever I dip my dark brush.
I have loved, and been loved in return, by solitude.
Back fifty feet in the pines,
All color relents,
And the quietness there, the stern quietness,
                                    is hard as stone.

———

At my age, memories scatter like rain
                        when one sits still, first day of summer,
The noise of the world
                    over a hundred miles away,
Sun sinking, but not as soon as yesterday, birds flown.

———

What does one do when you find out your thoughts
                              are the thoughts of everyone else?
Wait for a monk to come down
From his hill,
Look hard for the people whose lives you cannot explain,
Walk slowly under the shagbark trees?
I can't know, but as one ages
                         it comes as a matter of some reflection.

There are worse desolations, of course.
                              Abandoned cities, for one thing,
The thousand miles that stretch out
From one image to the next.
We all hum our own sad songs.
Make yours your favorite, and don't look
At the new grass, at the summer sun
                         in its dangling descent.

                         ▬

Light falls on the deer and the jump weed,
Light out my west window,
                         June light, the Sundown Special.
We know where she's headed—
                         your seat is used, but reserved.

                         ▬

This is the entry of evening light.
Where I am, it seems, it's always just before sunset.
At least nowadays,
Even in memory—
                    Lake Garda and Mykonos,
Venice, of course, and every place one can stand
                                        upon the abiding earth.
Local color still deep in the heart.
O my, as I said one time, I love to see that evening sun go down.

All the little black bugs have left the dandelions,
The robins have gone.
Even the clouds have changed
                    to the color of 2% milk.
Out the north window, the grasses stand bright and erect as acolytes.
I remember the way they stood at Desenzano, like that,
Some forty-five years ago,
Though I didn't pay much attention then,
                    twenty-three, on my way to anywhere else.

We're always, apparently, on our way to anywhere else,
And miss what we're here for,
                    the objects we never realize
Will constitute our desire,
The outtakes and throwaways of the natural world.
The movement of creek water at dusk,
The slippage and slow disappearance of what we love

Into the silence of here-and-now
                    that will survive us, and call back.

                    ———

The barn house is upside down in the motionless pond.
And pine trees.
                    Two ducks land suddenly
And everything's carried away in blurred, colorful pieces.

The summer passing of the black-sailed familiar,
The ghost bier of the Hunter Gracchus,

                    myth-driven, ill at ease,

Two-masted and low, is now at hand.
A wrong turn, a lack of attention,

               a lack, it seems, of love,

Has set its last course.
Like the four seasons, it wheels on the rings of air forever.

When the body is old, the heart becomes older still.

One needs no Paradise when the rain falls,
　　　　　　　and clouds are not scattered by the wind.
No one's around, the grasses bend at their belt buckles,
Boughs droop and the rain keeps coming down.
There is an edgy serenity in solitude,
　　　　　　　when the rain falls and the wind stops,
The perpetual presence of absence, where all things are still.

Rain over everything like sunlight,
　　　　　　　out of the clouds.
Shining in strings and beads, a giant hush,
Like tongues in the afterlife.
Clouds like the smoky aftereffect of forest fires,
High-drift and hang.
　　　　　　　Out of the stillness, a small splendor.

　　　　　　　———

The line between heaven and earth is a grass blade,
　　　　　　　a light green and hard to walk.

　　　　　　　———

Bigfoot, the north wind, slaps through the trees
Looking for something that we can't know,
　　　　　　　or even, perhaps, have heard of,

Pushing the boughs aside,

                          always gone, just out of sight.

Sunlight fills in his footprints.

After the answer, there's always another question,

Even the last one.

                    At least we have that to count on.

I am an image picker.

I like the ripe ones,

                  the ones at the ends of the listing limbs.

To know one's self is the final yes, of course.

                        The no,

However, is right behind it, and just as final.

How easy to lose oneself in the orchard,

                    this tree and that,

Everything shiny, everything slick and close to hand.

The evening prepares for the invisible,

                    the absence of itself.

Clouds defuse. White cat on the fence pole

Haunched on her throne.

                    Bird feathers glued to the window glass

Where finch attempted his noon flight through the visible.

Better to keep your head down,

                    asleep in the darkening trees.

Nothing can stop it. One sweep of its cape and it's gone.

―――

The morning is almost silent and cannot declare itself.
Therefore, I say unto it,
                    you are the never-boring miracle
Of sunlight and scrappy cloud,
The absence of rain when rain is absent,
                    as it is
This morning, green with its wonderment,
Last night's hard frost a wet memory
Scattered in bits and glitzy pieces
                    deep in the grass.

The ten horses of the field are like
                    the cities of the plain,
A necessary moment
Of everything that is, and was, and will be again,
Standing in succulence in the brevity of time.
The sunlight grows big,
                    immensity
Of noon approaching, its spurs flashing and its saber on fire.
The green backs off a bit, and mumbles. And so do we.

―――

I have nothing to say. I am a recording machine,
                    a listening device.
What I hear is what I will tell you.

I am the sluice of dead scrolls and songs,
                              I am the tongue of what exists,
Whose secrets are whispered and not heard.
Listen to me, listen to what's the nothing I have to say.

—

The shadows of the floating world
                              huddle beneath their objects.
Slowly, like hands on a massive clock,
They soon will begin their crawl and creep
                                   to bring us back
Tick-tock in their black sack, tick-tock in their soft black sack.

—

Lord of the Sunlight,
                    Lord of the Leftover, Lord of the Yet-To-Do,
Handle my heaven-lack, hold my hand.

The little birds are honing their beaks on the chopping block stump.
The clouds have gathered for their convention
                              from deep out in the dark Pacific.
They clear their throats and speak out.
Everything stills and listens,
                              even the little birds
With their sharp beaks and sharp claws,
                              clinging inside the tamaracks
Until the storm passes and the cloud bodies adjourn.

That's when the big birds come,
                    with their sweeping wings and dangling legs,
Their eyes ajar, and the lightning sparks from their keening claws.
The poppies along the near hill glisten like small fires,
Pink and orange and damp red.
Behind the glass window, we hear the swoosh of the giant wings,
And listen hard for the next pass,
                              but they don't come back.

It's not such a poverty, we think,
                              to live in a metaphysical world.
Thus we become poor, and spurn the riches of the earth.
Such nonsense.

The crow flies with his beak open,

                              emitting a raucous cry.

The yearling horses stand in the field,

                        up to their knees in the new grass.

This is the first world we live in, there is no second.

                        ▬

The mind's the affliction,

                      asleep for a hundred years,

Nothing to wake it but memory,

The deep blank of memory,

                       rivers and hills, the morning sun,

Simple things,

               the body moving, not much, but moving.

                        ▬

Orpheus walked, the poets say, down to the black river.

Nobody recognized him,

Of course, and the boat came,

                      the gondola with its singular oarsman,

And the crowd got in, a thousand souls,

So light that the boat drew no water, not even a half inch.

On the other side, the one paved road, and they took it.

Afterward, echoes of the great song webbed in their ears,

They took the same road back to the waiting gondola,

The two of them,

               the first to have ever returned to the soot-free shore.

The oarsman's stroke never faltered, and he hummed the song
He had caught the faint edges of
                              from the distant, marble halls.
It won't work, he thought to himself, it won't work. And it didn't.

—

Clouds, like the hills of heaven,
Are nowhere in evidence tonight.
                              Sundown, an empty sky.
Except for the quarter moon, like a sail with no ship,
And no home port to come to.
                              Its world is without end.

—

The smallest cloud I've ever seen
                              floats like a white midge
Over the western ridgeline,
Then vanishes in the wind and the dying sunlight.
How unremarkable,
                  though no moon comes to shine on its going out.
And nothing arrives to take its place.
Forlorn evening, that makes me want to sit here forever, and then
    some.
I'll likely meet it again, a thousand years from now,
When it rises up through my bedroom,
                              buzzing against the windowpane.

We are the generations of the soil,

> it is our cloak and put-on.

Somnambulistas of sore intent,

Barefoot or full-shod, it is our destination,

> our Compostela.

We rub its rock for luck, and slip inside to get warm,

As though, like our grandfathers before us,

> we lie down in our own hearts.

———

The dogs are barking under the newly planted trees.

When we're transplanted, they'll bark again,

> but not for us.

I never tire of watching the mists rise

                               under the mountain

After the rain, like a small detail

On a Chinese screen.

                   The overcast, usually,

Is starting to break, like this evening,

Into its horizontal whites and grays and scrimmed blues.

The mists invisibly come together and dissipate, come

Together and dissipate.

I never get tired of watching this,

As the mists seem to move, then not move.

They don't, of course, but merely disappear.

                              Perhaps that's why I like it.

The light is flat and hard and almost nonexistent,

The way our lives appear to us,

                    then don't, as our inlook shifts.

The horses know nothing of any of this, their heads in the wet grass.

And you know nothing of this, asleep, as you are, in the distant field.

Asleep, as you always will be, in the distant field.

                    ——

I've always loved, as Auden called them, the chinks in the forest,

(He had the deer peer through them)

Those little slashes and blades
                    of sunlight cutting streaks
Between the trees, imperceptibly healing over
As sunset pulls back down its high road
And the dark bandages of dusk
                    are placed on the forest floor.
I love to watch them thrust and retreat,
                       blazing the trees,
Making a trail so full of light that no one can follow it.

—

I've looked at this landscape long enough,
                      time for another book.
One less endless, perhaps, a finitude to count on
And not this enduring verdancy
And chapterless blue.

Sometimes one feels the need of ordinary things,
                       flies
Carcasses along the windowsills, wasps
Resurgent under the eaves,
Dropped feathers, pine chips.
              Sometimes you've got to face the dog.

—

Just after the war (the Second World War), in Kingsport,
I started listening to music,

Local music, east Tennessee and southwest Virginia,
"Rock of Ages," "The Great Speckled Bird," "Life Is Like a
    Mountain Railroad."
Like all children, I just accepted things,
                                    and never puzzled them out.

But "The Great Speckled Bird" was a different lyric.
I never could quite imagine it,
Though the song never failed to move my feet to music.
The great wings shadowed my childhood,
                                    and still do, from time to time,
Darkening some. Then darkening more.

━━━

There are songs, we now know, to be sung on the other side of
    language.
Our tongues are not capable, however,
                                    our eyes can't trill in the dark.

━━━

Sometimes I feel I've already told
                                    every story I've ever heard,
Or even once heard about.
God knows, even those are short enough,
And not, in their narratives, deliciously slow and drawn out.
I think, I guess, that immanence isn't a story,

And can't be.
                    In truth, it isn't linguistic at all,
Or metalinguistic either, or any of that.
So stub out your pencil, Pilgrim,
                              and listen to what the wind repeats
As it starts and erases itself,
Unstoppable storyteller with nothing to say.
I'd like to cry out in its book,
                         especially when it stalls,
On that blank page between one narrative and the next.

                         ▬

In the darkness between the tamaracks,
                         the light is bundled like little sticks,
Like fatwood for the fire about to start with the evening's match.

A word to the wise is a word to the wise,

       and isn't sufficient
To anything in this world.
Give me a thing that says nothing.

      The wind, for instance,
A wisdom that comes from ten thousand miles to the west.
The trees, for instance, stenographers
Of every sentence it isn't able to utter.
The grass that assembles them all

       in its green pages.
The dirt that subtracts each word, syllable after syllable,
Into its dark book, and keeps them there
In ignorance, a blessed ignorance we'll come to know,
A radiant cloud at our mouths,

      breath like no other.

Whoever would lay a seed of truth on the table
Had best have his left foot in the stirrup

       and both hands
On the saddle, and be good to go.
The wise is without wisdom, and that's as it should be,
So many words, so many.
The truth is another matter, and is, like wisdom,

As speechless as bull clover.
Outside, in the sun, Yugo the dog lies quietly,
His head on his paws.
What he sees he can't say,
                    but he sees what you see and I see.
His look is pure and pitiless and not on the what's-to-come.

                    ⎯

The little finches have come and gone
                    back to their tree.
They lay these words on my eyelids, grains of sleep.
                    Look for me, witness, look for me.

                    ⎯

The one-legged metal-green rooster
Nailed to the wall of the old chicken house
                    is all that remains
Of Snuffy Bruns, at least in these parts.
A small wooden platform where Beryl, his wife (his sister
As well, it turned out), would feed Marcia,
A pine squirrel she'd almost domesticated,
                    who would come when called,
Rots on a spruce tree by the outhouse.
He called me Easy Money—I liked that—and made the best knives
You're likely to come across.
Of the two, he died first, and early, much liked by all of us.
And Beryl was taken in downriver

By some family we didn't know well.
They came from Colorado, I think.
I loved his toothless grin and his laid-back ways.

                                  They shipped him there,
Careful truck driver to the end, after the last handshake and air-kiss,
From one big set of mountains to another, in a slow rig.

—

Tonight the ravens are dominant,
                          and whoosh the air
With their wings like oars on a black boat.
Who's dead, who's dead, they croak,
                             going from tree to tree limb,
Five of them, six of them, looking for blood and a place to land.
Not me, I mutter, not me.
Four ducks take off in loose formation like fighter planes.
Not them either, apparently.
                    So long, ducks, so long,
Ravens resting a moment above the pond,
                             and then they're gone,
The evening as still and tranquil as the inside of a bone
Till they return. And return they will,
Looking for what's available and warm, and what's not.
We live in their shadow, and under it,
                        and our days are long.

—

Don't sit by the side door, waiting for hangnail and radiance,
The past is a yellow dust.

Do what the wind does,
And let your life be heavier: no darkness, no light.

                        —

The birds keep flying into the windows.
                         They see the sky reflected
And keep on breaking their necks.
The birds keep flying into the windows.
                     They see the reflection of the sky.

The level's so low in the short pond,
The snipe seems to walk on water,
                              ruffling his dagger-drawn wings
As he heads for the next mossed hillock.
Suddenly, under a cloud, the sun's bottom auras the pond's surface,
And snipe is consumed by fire,
                    still walking, angelic, wings dipped in flame.
It must have been like this on the first retelling, back there on the
    long water,
Such mystery,
    sunlight and surface-shine and something winged on the waves,
Snipe settled now, deep beak in the curls.

The logo is Fra Angelico,
                              alone in the unfinished rooms
Upstairs in S. Marco, blank windows
He colored with apparitions and visitations,
The outlines already there,
Apparently, waiting to be filled in.
                              And he filled them, stroke by stroke,
Bringing the outside inside.
He painted, it's been said, the first recognizable landscape.

As for the others,
                he gathered the form from the air, and gave it flesh.

           ——

The snipe stands on top of himself
                on the water beneath him.
When he drinks, he drinks from his own mouth.
What could be luckier, as full of grace and replenishment,
As feeding oneself on one's other self, one's stand-in,
Life's little helper swagged under our feet,
                one's doppelgänger and replica?

Windless, just-August evening.
Only the grasses move, and slightly,
The tall grasses, hearing the whispers of gravity,
And turning their tired necks
                as though they'd prefer not to.
Otherwise, not even the stubbed clover moves, nor the snipe,
                either of them.

           ——

August, blue mother, is calling her children in
                soundlessly
Out of the sun-dried thistles
And out of the morning's dewlessness.
All of the little ones,
              the hard-backed and flimsy-winged,

The many-legged and short-of-breath,
She calls them all, and they come.

Listen, this time I think she's calling your name as well.

⸺

I wish I remembered the way the stars looked
                              up here some thirty-five years ago
When the lights went out.
Pretty much as they do now, I'd guess,
Though I never see them,
                         given, as now I am, to an early bed.
Original oxymorons, ice on fire, I loved to watch them fall.

And loved them, too, as they stayed in place,
Designs from the afterlife of dreams,
                                  and beyond that,
Connecting the dots of nothingness.
It comforts me to know they're up there,
                              and that their light
Keeps coming long after my sleep has gone forth, and my sleep's
    sleep.

⸺

We've all led raucous lives,
                        some of them inside, some of them out.
But only the poem you leave behind is what's important.

Everyone knows this.

The voyage into the interior is all that matters,

Whatever your ride.

Sometimes I can't sit still for all the asininities I read.

Give me the hummingbird, who has to eat sixty times

His own weight a day just to stay alive.

                                Now that's a life on the edge.

        ―――

I live here accompanied by clouds

Now that the weather's broken.

They take and release sunlight

                        like stained glass outside my small window.

A light that sometimes prompts me to want

To leave the world and settle, like some white bird,

                                on another mountain.

What does it profit us to say
The stiff new bristles of the spruce tree
Glisten like bottle brushes after the rain shower?
To what avail is the thunderstorm
Passing just north of us, and south too,
Like a growling and wire-haired dog

      still wishing us harm?
Description and metaphor,
The fancy dancing of language,

     to what good end, my friend, to what end?
And who will remember us and our enterprise,
Whose fingers will sift our dust?

We'll never know, Horatio, we will never know.

    ▬

Cold snap, not even mid-August yet,
The little engines of change at work
Unexpectedly in the atmosphere

      as well as our lives,
The dragging, black-bellied clouds
That enter our blood from the wrong side of the compass,
The double-clutch of wind-shift

Into off-limits and unappeasable places
Is coming our way soon,
    and slow-dropped out of the blue.
One sees it and feels it at the same time,
      noiselessly
Pulling toward the meridian, then over the hill.

     ——

The evening's homily comes down to this in the end:
Praise for the left-out and left-behind,
Praise for the left-over and over-looked,
      praise for the left hand
And the horse with one lame leg,
Praise for the going-down,
    and the farther going-down,
Praise for the half-things, red moon and the smoke-scented sky,
The bling and the left half of the heart,
The half-winded whicker of geldings,
      light water on top of the dark,
The dispossession of all landscape
As night cuts the music off,
    and pulls the plug and eases in.

     ——

The overheated vocabulary of the sun
Has sunk to just a few syllables,
    fewer than yesterday.

And fewer still tomorrow, I'd bet.

Slaphappy sidekick, guttering old fool,

tongue-tied and toasty,

What are your last ones likely to be, "you"? Or will they be "the"?

—

Bringing the horses in is like

bringing the past of the whole race in.

Sundown, a cloud-flittered sky.

They'd like blood, but hay is what they get,

Ghosts from our former lives,

ghosts who could carry us still.

Breathe lightly into their nostrils, scorgle their muzzles.

They brought us here,

and someday they'll take us far away.

—

Twenty hours of rain in the middle of August,

No thunder, no lightning strikes.

A gift.

I saw two kingfishers last week outside my window,

Above the creek. I hope they'll come back.

Autumn is under way, already the first gears

notched and turned.

—

Abandoned squirrel nest under cloud-slide.

Pencil stub.

The dread of what we can see, and the dread of what we can't see,
Crawl in the same manner,

one in back of the other.

——

Struck by the paucity of my imagination
To winnow the meadow from anything that it is,
I watch the yellow-tail hawk

cruising its edges, the willows

Along the creek's course,
Low down and lethal, then up like a slung lariat
To circle and telescope,
Eventually to noose back down
And crumble,

only to rise, big wings pumping, back to the west.

Beside me, the shadow of the wind chime's bamboo drag
Turns like a fish on a string
Noiselessly in the still waters of morning's sunlight.
A pack train of white and off-white clouds
Works east where the hawk had been.

Almost noon, the meadow

Waiting for someone to change it into an other. Not me.
The horses, Monte and Littlefoot,

Like it the way it is.

         And this morning, so do I.

—

After the end of something, there comes another end,
This one behind you, and far away.
Only a lifetime can get you to it,

         and then just barely.

The page is dark, and the story line is darker still.
We all have the same book,

                    identically inscribed.

We open it at the appointed day, and begin to read.

There is a kind of depression that empties the soul.
The eyes stay bright,
                    the mind stays clear as Canada on an autumn day
Just after the rain.
But the soul hangs loose as a plastic bag in a tree
When the wind has died.
                              It is that drained.
And overcast. The little jack-weeds
That line its edges exhale,
And everything falls to a still, uneasy remove.
It stirs when the wind shifts,
                              and seasons tumble and stall.
It stirs, but it doesn't disappear.
Though weeds re-up and the clouds relent,
                              it doesn't disappear.

―――

Like a golden Afro, a bunch of eidergrass has blossomed
And paled out
On top of an uprooted pine stump
Across the creek.
                    As the sun goes down,
What small light there is drains off into its spikiness,
And glows like a severed head against the darkness.

———

Oil lamp lit, outside light a similitude,
                              wet world
From recent downpour,
I think of you back in Massachusetts,
                              hurting from head to foot heel,
Still summer there, autumn beginning here, no drop of complaint.

———

Brushstroke, bullrushes in front of pond's mirror,
                                        rain spots
Pimpling diminished mountain.
My seventieth birthday,
                    such wonderful weather.

———

Whatever lights there are are ours, or can be,
                                  all things
We see are like that.
And those we can't see gather the light
                              closely unto themselves,
And look around steadily for us.
How is it we miss their messages?

———

August the 25th, the snipe gone.

                    Do they go south?

I suppose they must, but where?

Certainly not to east Tennessee,

Where I held the bag for hours

                    in Oak Ridge one evening after supper

(There goes the kingfisher, and then the yellow-tail hawk,

One up the creek, the other one down).

I hope they are walking now on a warmer water,

And that their reflections are just as clear,

                        and the moss as green.

Sixty-two years ago, the year of aluminum pennies,

My hands still burning,

                the mouth of that croker sack still open.

—

Lord, when the world is still, how still it is,

                    contrails and mare's tails

Crisscrossing the sky,

Patterned so lightly on its unmistakable air.

One waits for a presence from the darkening woods,

                    one large and undiminished,

But only its absence appears, big as all get-out.

Evening arrives so swiftly these days

                  even the weak-kneed weeds

Don't know which direction to bow in,
The fugitive wind-fingers,
Groping north, groping south,
                    then hanging like unstruck chimes
From their disused and desolate hands.

Out over the sunlit Pacific
Mischief is in the making
                    (Good, there's the kingfisher again,
Then gone in a blue, acetylene flash
Down to the trout horde),
Whose scratches and plum knots
                    we'll feel in a day or two.

                                     —

The world's whinny and the world's bit
                    are two thousand miles away.
How is it I hear its hoofbeats so sharp in my ear?

Emptiness happens.

                It's like the down-curving dead branch

On the pine tree outside my window

Which ends in nothing, its mossy beard

Moving just slightly, no more than that, in the slight wind.

One hopes, in due time, to be so moved,

                            in just such a garment.

There's an easy emptiness, and a hard emptiness,

The first one knowable, the second one not,

                     though some are said to have seen it

And come back to fight the first.

Which is bespoke, and fits like a shirt.

The second one's colorless, and far away,

                    as love is, or a resurrection.

                ———

The bottles my messages are sent in have long disappeared.

Cloudy September jumbles the sky.

The great purity waits for me,

               but no one has answered my questions.

                ———

These are the night journals,

                      an almanac of the afterhour,

Icarus having fallen

A long time ago, the sun in its ghostly pursuit

Behind him behind the ridge,

Not enough light to see the page,

                          not really,

Much less to imagine how it must have been, the pale boy

Scalded by burning wax,

                    cooled by wind,

The water a sudden oblivion, so nothing, so welcoming,

So many worlds since then, all of them so alike, all of them

Suncatcher, father and son.

                   —

The beginning of autumn dark is quick, and it's cold, and long.

My time of life is a preen of feathers, and goes on and on.

If not in me, then in you,

                  cousin.

I'll look for you in the deep light, on the other side.

The water is wadable,

                not too big, not too small.

I'll be the one with white hair, avoiding the mirror.

                  —

It's odd how certain combinations

                      are carved twice in the memory,

Once in the surface riprap and once in the deep seams.
Lake Garda is like that, and Valpolicella wine,
The sun going down above Salò,
The waters, as has been said,
                        crumpling and smoothing toward Bardolino,
Fish on the grill, the wine like blood in liter carafes,
The dusk a darkish serenity laying its hands
On our shoulders
                        warmly, with a touch of freshness, but warmly.
When you're twenty-three, you'll live forever, a short time.

—

One horse up and one horse down.
                                And Punta S. Vigilio,
Olive trees semaphoring in the wind O love me.
And I did, I did.
                    I wonder if I will ever see it again?
And Riva, that myth-bag, Gardone,
And all the way over and back to Sirmione?
And Thorpe and Hobart and Schimmel and Schneeman,
                                            will I see them,
And Via Mazzini, La Greppia, Piazza Erbe?
Not as they were and not as I was.
The past is a dark disaster, and no one returns.
Initials are left, and dates.
Sometimes the bodies are still hanging,
                        and sometimes not.

Hark, hark, the dogs do bark;
The poets are coming to town.
One in rags and one in tags,
And one in a silken gown.

Backyard, my old station, the dusk invisible in the trees,
But there in its stylish tint,
Everything etched and precise before the acid bath
—Hemlocks and hedgerows—
Of just about half an hour from now,
Night in its soak and dissolve.
Pipistrello, and gun of motorcycles downhill,
A flirt and a gritty punctuation to the day's demise
And one-starred exhalation,
                                      V of geese going south,
My mind in their backwash, going north.

The old gospel song from 1950
                                      by Lester Flatt and Earl Scruggs,
"Reunion in Heaven," has a fugitive last verse
I must have heard once
Although it wasn't included when they recorded it.
So I'll list it here,
                    that it won't be disremembered.
Just in case.
I am longing to sit by the banks of the river
There's rest for the ones by the evergreen trees

I am longing to look in the face of my Savior
And my loved ones who have gone, they are waiting for me

⸻

When what you write about is what you see,
                    what do you write about when it's dark?
Paradise, Pound said, was real to Dante because he saw it.
Nothing invented.
One loves a story like that, whether it's true or not.
Whenever I open my eyes at night, outside,
                                flames edge at the edge
Of everything, like the sides of a nineteenth-century negative.
If time is a black dog, and it is,
Why do I always see its breath,
                        its orange, rectangular breath
In the dark?
It's what I see, you might say, it's got to be what my eyes see.

⸻

So many joys in such a brief stay.
Life is a long walk on a short pier.

⸻

If poetry is pentimento,
                    as most of its bones seem to show,
Remember the dead deer on Montana 92,

Lincoln County, last Monday, scrunched in the left-hand ditch.
Raven meat-squawks for two days.
On Thursday, south wind through the rib cage,
Ever-so-slightly a breathing,
                              skull-skink unmoved on the macadam.
Its song was somewhat, somewhat erased.

I'm early, no one in the boat on the dark river.
It drifts across by itself
Below me.
          Offended, I turn back up the damp steps.

The dragonflies remain a great mystery to me.
Early October.
                    At least a dozen of them are swarming
Like swallows over the dying grass
And browned leaves of the backyard,
Each tending to recompose a previous flight path
With minor variations.
So beautiful,
              translucent wings against the translucent sky,
The late afternoon like litmus just under our fingertips.

The berries shine like little stigmata in the dogwood trees,
A thousand reminders of the tree's mythology
As the rain keeps polishing them,

                      as though it could rub it clean.

Such red, and Easter so far away.

The song of someone like me
                         begins on the pennywhistle.
A few notes, just a few, up and down.
The bass line comes in,
                     then the lead and second guitar.
Brushstrokes on the snares.
And then the singer, Lord, then the singer steps up.
What voice could slip this backdrop?
Only the rise and fall of the newly damned, perhaps,
                       or the Great Speckled Bird.
Or some sough through the big larch limbs, some sibilance in the
    pines.
Little lost squawks in the natural world,
                       lost voices.
I gather them unto me, I become their mouthpiece.

Sordello, with lazy and honest eyes, still waits for us
Beyond the *palude* off Via Mantovana
Just this side of Sabbionetta,
His terraced, invisible mountain
Rising above Lake Garda into the infinite.

Not time for that hike yet, we hoped,
                                    feet hot on the cobblestones
In front of Palazzo Ducale.
Not yet, we hoped, our foreheads already feeling the sword's tip.
And angel wings.
                        You got to carry that weight for a long time,
And pray for the angel's wing
When the time comes, when the time does come.

                                    ▭

Moonlight like watery paint
On the yard grass and arborvitae.

Shadows like Franz Kline from the spruce trees.

Circle of neighbor's basketball goal like the entrance to Hell
On stone-spattered, leaf-littered driveway.

October, old ghost month, you outline my *fine del camin*.

                                    ▭

There is a photograph of Stan Hyman and me in our Army dress
    blues,
2nd Lieutenants, standing in front of a No Parking sign
In Pacific Grove, California, 1958.
There are a hundred million snapshots

Just like it, Stan's wedding day, the 24 August.
Mine means a world to me, a world never to return,
But one never left, if truth be told.
And yours? You have at least one, I know, just like it,
                          different people, different place,
But the same. What does it mean to you?
Who could imagine it would ever become like this?

—

All I have left undone, I hope someone will make good
In this life or the next,
                    whichever comes first. Or second.

—

Moon riseth not, as some Victorian must have said back in the day,
Stars like a motorcycle's exhaust
Through the limp leaves of the maple trees.
                          Not much excitement here,
Though headlights and taillights go back and
Forth like pine-pitch torches in some Attic procession,
The limbs of Orpheus overhead
At the front,
      his blue-tongued and pale head behind on the slow Rivanna,
Bumping from snag to sandbar, but singing, still singing.

—

The start of things, and the end of things,
Two unmarked graves,
                    the autumn wind rising west of the mountains.
Goodbye to the promise of What's Left.

———

The emptiness of nonbeing,
                    that which endures through all change—
Something to shoot for, for sure,
Something to seek out and walk on,
                    one footprint after the next.
In any case, after this life of who-knows-how-many years,
Who's not a shrunken, pitiable sight?

———

I empty myself with light
Until I become morning.

It's dark now, but I remember the five-fingered jaundiced leaves
Seeming to hover above the earth this afternoon
On the tips, the dull tips, of grass blades

                    under the maple tree,
The dogwood berries on Locust Avenue like scarlet cluster bombs,
Automobiles and ambulance sirens

                    cutting the sundown, October air,
Thinking, this isn't at all bad, not even one bit,
All the way to the hospital, and all the way back.
And now here's Mars, like a pancake orange,
Northeast in the bleached-star sky,

                    and that's not at all bad either,
End of October, end of a buffed and edgeless day.

          —

Halloween, All Hallows' Eve.

                And what if they came back,
All of them, what would we say?
That the moon looks good through the limbs of the chinaberry tree?
That the night air is as easy as oil on the skin?
That the children parading in their pathetic little costumes

                    have it right?
That the give in the natural world
Is as good as the take in the supernatural other?

That the moon looks good and the stars still refuse to shine?
What would we say, Slick, what would we say,
Our hands like skeletal party gloves,

                                   our masks future faces?

—

I think of the masters of a century ago,
And often wish they'd come and whisper their secrets in my ear,
My right ear, the good one. Not all, perhaps, but a couple.

The fallen leaves
                    litter the lawn and driveway. Autumn.
Indian summer. Nothing ripples.
The other side of the world, they say, is a door
                              where I'll find my life again.

—

New moon like a jai alai basket
                        just over the doctor's rooftop,
Cradling the old moon before her fall.

—

If angels can see into the ends and beginnings of things,
Why are they still among us
Like widowed birds, circling, circling,
                    their poor go-betweens at a full stop?

—

The cold gowns of the masters,

                              those of a thousand years ago,

Over a thousand, and then some,

Wander the countryside,

                    brushing like loose crystal against the sumac.

Who here can inhabit them?

Whose arms among us can fill their sleeves,

So clear and transparent, so radiant in the dark?

My neighbor's maple tree shines like a galleon in the dusk,

Kumquat and blood orange,

                        pomegranate and nectarine.

Within such splendor, everything falls away, even our names,

All trace of our being here, breathed in by the night's lips.

This is as close as we get to them,

Their tinkling crystal folds just ahead of us,

                                 how sweet a sound.

———

Is there an emptiness we all share?

                            Before the end, I mean.

Heaven and earth depend on this clarity,

                              heaven and earth.

Under the gold doubloons of the fallen maple leaves,

The underworld burrows in,

                    sick to death of the light.

When death shall close these eyelids,
And this heart shall cease to beat,
And they lay me down to rest
In some flowery-bound retreat.

Will you miss me, will you miss me,
Will you miss me,
Will you miss me when I'm gone?

Perhaps you'll plant a flower
On my poor, unworthy grave,
Come and sit alone beside me
When the roses nod and wave.

Will you miss me, will you miss me,
Will you miss me,
Will you miss me when I'm gone?

One sweet thought my soul shall cherish
When this fleeting life has flown,
This sweet thought will cheer when dying,
Will you miss me when I'm gone?

When these lips shall never more
Press a kiss upon thy brow,
But lie cold and still in death,
Will you love me then as now?

Will you miss me, will you miss me,
Will you miss me,
Will you miss me when I'm gone?

FROM

SESTETS

TOMORROW

The metaphysics of the quotidian was what he was after:
A little dew on the sunrise grass,
A drop of blood in the evening trees,

                    a drop of fire.

If you don't shine you are darkness.
The future is merciless,

                everyone's name inscribed
On the flyleaf of the Book of Snow.

FUTURE TENSE

All things in the end are bittersweet—
An empty gaze, a little way station just beyond silence.

If you can't delight in the everyday,
                                    you have no future here.
And if you can, no future either.

And time, black dog, will sniff you out,
                                    and lick your lean cheeks,
And lie down beside you—warm, real close—and will not move.

FLANNERY'S ANGEL

Lead us to those we are waiting for,
Those who are waiting for us.
May your wings protect us,

      may we not be strangers in the lush province of joy.

Remember us who are weak,
You who are strong in your country which lies beyond the thunder,
Raphael, angel of happy meeting,

      resplendent, hawk of the light.

IN PRAISE OF WHAT IS MISSING

When a tooth is extracted,
                    some side of the holy wheel is unnotched,
And twists, unlike Ixion's, in the wind and weather,
And one slips into wanting nothing more
                            from the human world,
And leans back, a drifting cloud,
Toward what becomes vacant and is nameless and is blue,
As days once were, and will be again.

BY THE WATERS OF BABYLON

We live on Orphan Mountain,
                    each of us, and that's how it is,
Kingfisher still wet
And chattering on his empty branch.

Water remains immortal—
Poems can't defile it,
                    the heron, immobile on one leg,
Stands in it, snipe stitch it, and heaven pillows its breast.

HASTA LA VISTA BUCKAROO

So many have come and gone, undone
like a rhinestone cowboy,
Dazzle and snuff, Lord, dazzle and snuff,
In a two-bit rodeo.

The entrance to Hell is just a tiny hole in the ground,
The size of an old pecan, soul-sized, horizon-sized.
Thousands go through it each day before the mist clears
thousands one by one you're next.

BORN AGAIN II

Take me down to the river,

                the ugly, reseasoned river.

Add on me a sin or two,

Then cleanse me, and wash me, O white-shirted Pardoner.

Suerte, old friend.

The caravan's come and gone, the dogs have stopped barking,

And nothing remains but the sound of the water monotonous,

                      and the wind.

NO ENTRY

It is not possible to imagine and feel the pain of others.

We say we do but we don't.

It is a country we have no passport for,

        and no right of entry.

Empathy is emphatic,

      and sends long lines across the floor.

But it's not the hurt or wound.

It's not the secret of the black raven,

        cut out by water into oblivion.

CELESTIAL WATERS

May 30th, early evening,
                              one duck on the narrow water, pond
Stocked with clouds,
The world reflected and windless, full of grace, tiny, tiny.

Osiris has shown us the way to cross the coming night sky,
The route, the currents, the necessary magic words.
Stick to your business, boys,
                       and forget the down-below.

Dun-colored moth past the windowpane.

                    Now, he's got the right idea,

Fuzzy and herky-jerky,

        little Manichaean

Pulled by invisible strings toward light wherever it is.

On the 5th of June, the mother is like a shining,

Blue raindrop the sunlight refracts

                 on the tip of the spruce tree,

Crack in the bulbous sky the moth is yo-yoed up to.

SUNLIGHT BETS ON THE COME

The basic pleasures remain unchanged,
                        and their minor satisfactions—
Chopping wood, building a fire,
Watching the elk herd
          splinter and cruise around the outcrop of spruce trees

As the deer haul ass,
              their white flags like synchronized swimmers' hands,
Sunlight sealing—stretched like Saran Wrap—
The world as we know it,
              keeping it fresh-flamed should tomorrow arrive.

"WELL, GET UP, ROUNDER,

LET A WORKING MAN LAY DOWN"

The kingdom of minutiae,
                           that tight place where most of us live,
Is the kingdom of the saved,
Those who exist between the cracks,
                           those just under the details.

When the hand comes down, the wing-white hand,
We are the heads of hair
                           and finger bones yanked out of their shoes,
We are the Rapture's children.

CONSOLATION AND THE

ORDER OF THE WORLD

There is a certain hubris,

                or sense of invulnerability,

That sends us packing

Whenever our focus drops a stop, or the flash fails.

These snaps are the balance of our lives,

Defining moments, permanent signs,

Fir shadows needling out of the woods,

                        night with its full syringe.

RETURN OF THE PRODIGAL

Now comes summer, water clear, clouds heavy with weeping.
Tall grasses are silver-veined.
Little puddles of sunlight collect
                              in low places deep in the woods.

Lupine and paintbrush stoic in ditch weed,
                         larch rust a smear on the mountainside.
No light on ridgeline.
Zodiac pinwheels across the heavens,
                              bat-feint under Gemini.

WITH HORACE, SITTING ON

THE PLATFORM, WAITING

FOR THE *ROBERT E. LEE*

Seventy years, and what's left?

                              Or better still, what's gone before?

A couple of lines, a day or two out in the cold?

And all those books, those half-baked books,

                              sweet yeast for the yellow dust?

What say, Orazio? Like you, I'm sane and live at the edge of things,

Countryside flooded with light,

Sundown,

   the chaos of future mornings just over the ridge, but not here yet.

THE EVENING IS TRANQUIL, AND

DAWN IS A THOUSAND MILES AWAY

The mares go down for their evening feed

into the meadow grass.

Two pine trees sway the invisible wind—

some sway, some don't sway.

The heart of the world lies open, leached and ticking with sunlight

For just a minute or so.

The mares have their heads on the ground,

the trees have their heads on the blue sky.

Two ravens circle and twist.

On the borders of heaven, the river flows clear a bit longer.

HOMAGE TO WHAT'S-HIS-NAME

Ah, description, of all the arts the least appreciated.
Well, it's just this and it's just that,

                         someone will point out.
Exactly. It's just this and it's just that and nothing other.

From landscape to unsuppressed conjunction, it's only itself.
No missteps, no misreading.

                     And what's more metaphysical than that,
The world in its proper posture, on all fours, drinking the sweet
    water?

TUTTI FRUTTI

"A-wop-bop-a-loo-lop a-lop-bam-boo,"

                            Little Richard in full gear—

What could be better than that?

Not much that I know of, at least not in my green time.

It's hard, O, my, it is hard,

To find a sustainable ecstasy, and make it endure.

Detail, detail, detail—God and the Devil

                          hang side by side between each break.

"THIS WORLD IS NOT MY HOME,

I'M ONLY PASSING THROUGH"

The more you say, the more mistakes you'll make,
                                        so keep it simple.
No one arrives without leaving soon.
This blue-eyed, green-footed world—
                        hello, Goldie, goodbye.

We won't meet again. So what?
The rust will remain in the trees,
                        and pine needles stretch their necks,
Their tiny necks, and sunlight will snore in the limp grass.

STILETTO

Why does each evening up here

                        always, in summer, seem to be

The way—as it does, with the light knifing low from right to left—

It will be on the next-to-last one?

The next-to-last one for me, I mean.

There is no music involved,

                   so it must be the light, and its bright blade.

The last one, of course, will be dark.

                          And the knife will be dark too.

"I SHALL BE RELEASED"

There is a consolation beyond nomenclature
                                    of what is past
Or is about to pass, though I don't know what it is.
But someone, somewhere, must, and this is addressed to him.

Come on, Long Eyes, crack the book.
Thumb through the pages and stop at the one with the golden script.
Breathe deeply and lay it on me,
                        that character with the luminous half-life.

DESCRIPTION'S THE ART

OF SOMETHING OR OTHER

Description is expiation,
                              and not a place to hunker down in.
It is a virtual world
Unfit for the virtuous.
                              It is a coming to terms with.

Or coming to terms without.
As though whatever we had to say could keep it real.
As though our words were flies,
                              and the dead meat kept reappearing.

"IT'S SWEET TO BE REMEMBERED"

No one's remembered much longer than a rock
                    is remembered beside the road
If he's lucky or
Some tune or harsh word
                    uttered in childhood or back in the day.

Still how nice to imagine some kid someday
                    picking that rock up and holding it in his hand
Briefly before he chucks it
Deep in the woods in a sunny spot in the tall grass.

IN MEMORY OF THE

NATURAL WORLD

Four ducks on the pond tonight, the fifth one MIA.
A fly, a smaller-than-normal fly,
Is mapping his way through sun-strikes across my window.

Behind him, as though at attention,
                              the pine trees hold their breaths.
The fly's real, the trees are real,
And the ducks.
                    But the glass is artificial, and it's on fire.

YELLOW WINGS

When the sun goes down—and you happen to notice it—
And the sky is clear, there's always a whitish light
                               edging the earth's offerings.
This is the lost, impermanent light
The soul is pulled toward, and longs for, deep in its cave,
Little canary.
This is the light its wings dissolve in
                        if it ever gets out from underground.

TWILIGHT OF THE DOGS

Death is the mother of nothing.
                            This is a fact of life,
And exponentially sad.
All these years—a lifetime, really—thinking it might be otherwise.

What are the colors of despair?
                            Are they calibrated, like vowels?
How will we know them?
Who knows where the light will fall
                            as the clouds go from west to the east?

REMEMBERING BERGAMO ALTA

A post-apocalyptic poetry
                    starts with a dog bite
And featherless birds in the ruined trees,
People nowhere to be found.

Mostly it has to do with cities,
                     and empty boulevards,
Chairs in the public parks with no one to sit in them.
Mostly it's wind in vacant spaces,
                  and piano chords from a high window.

All four of the ducks are gone now.

                               Only the mountain remains,

Upside down like Purgatorio
In the pond's reflection,

                no tree at the top, and no rivers.

No matter. Above it, in either incarnation,
The heavens, in all their golden numbers, begin to unstack.
Down here, as night comes on, we look for Guido,
    his once best friend, and Guido's father, and Bertran de Born.

WALKING BESIDE THE

DIVERSION DITCH LAKE

I love to make the kingfishers fly
                    from their bony perches
Above the lake, six or seven, one after the next,
Circling the water and chattering back,
                    as I walk along.

Can the fish hear them?
Is their cry like organ chording,
                    leading to one vast ultimate stop?
Who was it who first said, "The kingfisher falls through fire"?

NEXT

The Great Scribe, who remembers nothing,
                not even your name the instant he writes it down,
Would like it up here, I think,
The blank page of the sundown sky, the tamarack quill points,
                        and no one to answer for.

This would be a tough story to crack.
Who wouldn't embrace such an absence,
Especially someone whose page is always full,
                and whose narrative goes nowhere?

THE GHOST OF WALTER BENJAMIN

WALKS AT MIDNIGHT

The world's an untranslatable language
                              without words or parts of speech.
It's a language of objects
Our tongues can't master,
                    but which we are the ardent subjects of.

If *tree* is *tree* in English,
                    and *albero* in Italian,
That's as close as we can come
To divinity, the language that circles the earth
                    and which we'll never speak.

BEES ARE THE TERRACE

BUILDERS OF THE STARS

It's odd how the objects of our lives
Continue to not define us,

                no matter how close we hold them unto us.
Odd how the narrative of those lives is someone else's narrative.

Now the increasing sundown.

                The Bible draws the darkness around it,
No footbridge or boat over Lethe,
No staircase or stepping-stone

              up into the Into.

WHEN THE HORSES GALLOP AWAY

FROM US, IT'S A GOOD THING

I always find it strange—though I shouldn't—how creatures don't
    care for us the way we care for them.
Horses, for instance, and chipmunks, and any bird you'd name.
Empathy's only a one-way street.

And that's all right, I've come to believe.
It sets us up for ultimate things,

                      and penultimate ones as well.
It's a good lesson to have in your pocket when the Call comes to call.

AUTUMN IS VISIONARY,

SUMMER'S THE SAME OLD STUFF

Half-moon rising, thin as a contact lens.

                              The sun going down

As effortlessly as a body through deep water,

Both at the same time, simple pleasures

As autumn begins to rustle and rinse,

                      as autumn begins to prink.

And now the clouds come on,

                  the same clouds that Turner saw.

Half of the moon sees them, half does not.

BITTER HERBS TO EAT,

AND DIPPED IN HONEY

We lay out our own dark end,

              guilt, and the happiness of guilt.

God never enters into it, nor

Do his pale hands and pale wings,

              angel of time he has become.

The wind doesn't blow in the soul,

              so no boat there for passage.

Half paths of the half-moon, then,

To walk up and down in the forest,

              to walk hard in the bright places.

NO ANGEL

In the Kingdom of the Hollow-at-Heart, the insect is king.
In the Kingdom of the Beyond,
                          all lie where the ground is smooth.
Everything's what it seems to be, and a little less.

In the land of the unutterable,
                    words float like reflections across the water.
Nobody visits us here.
Like shadows, we spread ourselves until our hands touch,
                              then disappear in the dark.

TIME IS A GRACELESS

ENEMY, BUT PURLS AS

IT COMES AND GOES

I'm winding down. The daylight is winding down.
                              Only the night is wound up tight,
And ticking with unpaused breath.
Sweet night, sweet steady, reliable, uncomplicated night.

September moon, two days from full,
                              slots up from the shouldered hill.
There is no sound as the moon slots up, no thorns in its body.
Invisible, the black gondola floats
                    through down-lid and drowning stars.

What's up, grand architect of the universe?

                                  The stars are falling,

The moon is failing behind your vaporous laundry,

Planets are losing their names,

           and darkness is dropping inches beneath the earth.

Down here, we take it in stride.

The horses go on with their chomp and snatch in the long grasses,

The dogs cringe,

           and coyotes sing in the still woods, back out of sight.

BEFORE THE PROPANE LAMPS

COME ON, THE WORLD IS

A RISK AND WONDER

Sundown smoke like a pink snood
                                    over the gathered hair of the mountains,
The sun a garish hatpin
Incongruous in the netting and underfold of the day.

The creek's voice is constant,
                                    and like a shadow embraces many things.
I wish it were my voice, but it's not.
My voice is a human thing, and weak,
                                    and it disappears with the sun.

AUTUMN THOUGHTS

ON THE EAST FORK

Daytime is boredom after a while, I've come to find, and nighttime
    too.
But in between,
      when the evening starts to drain the seen world into the unseen,
And the mare's-tail clouds swish slowly across the mountains,

Contentment embraces me
With its spidery arms and its spade-tipped, engendering tail.
There must be a Chinese character for this, a simple one,
                    but we've never seen it up here.

ON THE NIGHT OF THE
FIRST SNOW, THINKING
ABOUT TENNESSEE

It's dark now, the horses have had their half apple,

mist and rain,

Horses down in the meadow, just a few degrees above snow.

I stand in front of the propane stove, warming my legs.

If the door were open, I'd listen to creek water
And think I heard voices from long ago,

distinct, and calling me home.

The past becomes such a mirror—we're in it, and then we're not.

OUR DAYS ARE POLITICAL, BUT

BIRDS ARE SOMETHING ELSE

Tenth month of the year.
                              Fallen leaves taste bitter. And grass.
Everything that we've known, and come to count on,
                                             has fled the world.
Their bones crack in the west wind.

Where are the deeds we're taught to cling to?
How I regret having missed them,
                              and their mirrored pieces of heaven.
Like egrets, they rise in the clear sky,
                       their shadows like distance on the firred hills.

WE HOPE THAT LOVE

CALLS US, BUT SOMETIMES

WE'RE NOT SO SURE

No wind-sighs. And rain-splatter heaves up over the mountains,
                                                and dies out.
October humidity
Like a heart-red tower light,
                    now bright, now not so bright.

Autumn night at the end of the world.
In its innermost corridors,
                    all damp and all light are gone, and love, too.
Amber does not remember the pine.

TIME IS A DARK CLOCK,

BUT IT STILL STRIKES

FROM TIME TO TIME

Whump-di-ump-whump-whump,
                              tweedilee tweedilee tweedilidee,
I'm as happy as can be . . .
Pretty nice, but that was then,
                    when our hearts were meat on the grill.

And who was it, Etta James or Ruth Brown or LaVern Baker?
The past is so dark, you need a flashlight to find your own shoes.
But what shoes! and always half an inch off the floor,
                    your feet like wind inside them.

LIKE THE NEW MOON,

MY MOTHER DRIFTS

THROUGH THE NIGHT SKY

Beyond the boundaries of light and dark,
                           my mother's gone out and not come back.
Suddenly now, in my backyard, like the slip moon she rises
And rests in my watching eye.

In my dreams she's returned just like this, over a hundred times.
She knows what I'm looking for,
Partially her,
            partially what she comes back not to tell me.

AS THE TRAIN ROLLS THROUGH,

I REMEMBER AN OLD POEM

Well, here we are again, old friend, Ancient of Days,
Eyeball to eyeball.
I blink, of course,

                    I blink more than ten thousand times.

Dear ghost, I picture you thus, eventually like
St. Francis in his hair shirt,

                    naked, walking the winter woods,
Singing his own song in the tongue of the troubadours.

APRIL EVENING

Spring buzz-cut on the privet hedge,
                                    a couple of yellow cups
Downdrafting from the honeysuckle.
One bird in the hapless holly tree,
                                    giving us liftoff and glide.

It is amazing how beautiful springtime can be,
Bell jar over our ills and endless infirmities,
Transparancy into where we know
                                    the light will never reach us.

THE BOOK

Whose name will be inscribed in the book
                                        just before mine?
From what country, from what unburiable ever?
Somebody I'll never know, for sure,
Somebody whose fingers will never outline my face.

A splinter of his death will always remain in mine,
However,
            no matter how thick, no matter how thin.

SUNDOWN BLUES

There are some things that can't be conveyed—
                                        description, for instance,
The sundown light on that dog-hair lodgepole pine
                              and the dead branches of spruce trees.

They hold its brilliance close against them
For a tick or two
                    before it chameleons away.
No one is able to describe this gold to bronze to charcoal, no one.
So move along, boy, just move along.

"ON THE TRAIL OF

THE LONESOME PINE"

The older I become, the more the landscape resembles me.
All morning a misty rain,
All afternoon the sun uncovered and covered by cloud snares.

At night, in the evergreens,
The moonlight slides off the wind-weary branches, and will
    not stick.
No movement, the dark forest.

NO DIRECTION HOME

After a certain age, there's no one left to turn to.
You've got to find Eurydice on your own,

                                           you've got

To find the small crack

                    between here and everywhere else all by yourself.

How could it be otherwise?
Everyone's gone away, the houses are all empty,
And overcast starts to fill the sky like soiled insulation.

HOVERCRAFT

Hummingbird stopped as a period, breast embossed
                                        purple-pink-crimson
Outside the northside window,
Wings invisible in their stillness,
                          unquiet, never faltering.

And then, whoosh, he's gone,
Leaving a little hole in the air, one that the air
                                doesn't rush in to fill.
Empty pocket.
              The world, and the other world, are full of them.

TIME IS A CHILD-BITING DOG

Like rivers, my thoughts flow south,

                                 for no particular reason.

Must be the full moon

That floods the sky, and makes the night wakeful

                                      and full of remorse.

It's not here yet, but give it an hour or so, then we,

Bewildered, who want our poems to be clouds

                                upholding the sour light of heaven,

Will pass our gray hair through our fingers

                                      and sigh just a little bit.

NOTHING IS WRITTEN

In a couple of hours, it will start all over again,
The stars will lean down and stare from their faceless spaces,
And the moon will boot up on the black screen of the sky,
                                humping toward God-knows-what,

And we, with our pinched mouths and pinched eyes, the next
    morning
Will see its footprint like a slice of snow
                                torn off over Caribou,
Looking for somewhere else to be born.

LITTLE ENDING

Bowls will receive us,

                     and sprinkle black scratch in our eyes.

Later, at the great fork on the untouchable road,

It won't matter where we have become.

Unburdened by prayer, unburdened by any supplication,

Someone will take our hand,

                     someone will give us refuge,

Circling left or circling right.

A Short History of the Shadow

LOOKING AROUND III: Osip Mandelstam, *Selected Poems*, translated by Clarence Brown and W. S. Merwin (New York: New York Review of Books Classics, 2004).

IF MY GLASSES WERE BETTER, I COULD SEE WHERE I'M HEADED FOR: Carter Family, "The Pilgrim Slippers" (trad.).

IS: Annie Dillard, *For the Time Being* (New York: Knopf, 1999).

POLAROIDS: Osip Mandelstam, *Selected Poems*; Georg Trakl, *Poems*, translated by Lucia Cordell Getsi (Athens, GA: Mundus Artium, 1973).

RELICS: Aldo Buzzi, "Notes on Life," in Aldo Buzzi and Ann Goldstein, *A Weakness for Almost Everything: Notes on Life, Gastronomy, and Travel* (Hanover, NH: Steerforth, 1999).

NINE-PANEL YAAK RIVER SCREEN: Georg Trakl, *Poems*; Osip Mandelstam, *Selected Poems*.

BODY AND SOUL II: Richard Bernstein, *Ultimate Journey: Retracing the Path of an Ancient Buddhist Monk Who Crossed Asia in Search of Enlightenment* (New York: Vintage, 2001).

Buffalo Yoga

BUFFALO YOGA: Georg Trakl, *Poems*; "L'Ame de Napoléon, 1912," by Leon Bloy, in Jorge Luis Borges, *Selected Non-Fictions*, ed. Eliot Weinberger (New York, Penguin Books, 1999). Tom Andrews (1961–2001): "Alles Nahe werde fern" (Goethe).

ROSSO VENEXIANO:

    BERRYMAN: Well, being a poet is a funny kind of jazz. It doesn't get you anything. It doesn't get you any money, or not much, and

it doesn't get you any prestige, or not much. It's just something
you *do*.

INTERVIEWER: Why?

BERRYMAN: That's a tough question. I'll tell you a real answer. I'm
taking your question seriously. This comes from Hamann, quoted
by Kierkegaard. There are two voices, and the first voice says,
"Write!" and the second voice says, "For whom?" I think that's
marvelous; he doesn't question the imperative, you see that. And
the first voice says, "For the dead whom thou didst love." Again the
second voice doesn't question it; instead it says, "Will they read
me?" And the first voice says, "Aye, for they return as posterity."
Isn't that good?

—John Berryman, *Antæus* 8 (Winter 1973)

IN PRAISE OF HAN SHAN: *Mountain Home.*

Scar Tissue

WRONG NOTES: Witter Bynner, *The Jade Mountain: A Chinese An-
thology, Being Three Hundred Poems of the T'ang Dynasty, 618–906*,
translated by Witter Bynner from the texts of Kiang Kang-Hu (New
York, Knopf, 1957).

HERACLITEAN BACKWASH: Heraclitus, *Fragments*, translated by
Brooks Haxton (New York: Penguin Books, 2001).

MATINS: *Wu Wei*—In Taoism and Zen Buddhism, unmotivated action;
in Chinese, literally, "nondoing." (Robert Denham in *Northrop Frye
Unbuttoned* [Frankfort, KY: Gnomon Press, 2004].)

VESPERS: Hildegard of Bingen, *Selected Writings*, translated by Mark
Atherton (New York: Penguin Books, 2001).

HAWKSBANE: Matsuo Bashō, *The Narrow Road to the Deep North and
Other Travel Sketches*, translated by Nobuyuki Yuasa (New York: Pen-
guin Books, 1966).

Littlefoot

2: *Nag Hammadi Library*, James M. Robinson, general editor (New York: Harper & Row, 1978).

9: W. G. Sebald, "Dr. K. Takes the Waters at Riva," in *Vertigo* (New York: New Directions, 1999).

10: For Wilma Hammond.

11: *Returning Home, Tao-Chi's Album of Landscapes and Flowers*, introduction and commentaries by Wen Fong (New York: George Braziller, 1976).

17: *Mountain Home*, translated by David Hinton (Berkeley, CA: Counterpoint, 2002).

18: Ryan Fox, Sonny Rollins.

20: Elizabeth Kolbert in *The New Yorker*, June 2005.

20: *Poems of Wang Wei*, translated by G. W. Robinson (New York: Penguin Classics, 1973).

23: *The Collected Poems of Wallace Stevens* (New York: Knopf, 1954).

33: Giuseppe Ungaretti, "Mattino."

34: Bob Dylan, "It Takes a Lot to Laugh, It Takes a Train to Cry."

35: A. P. Carter, "Will You Miss Me When I'm Gone."

Sestets

CELESTIAL WATERS: Roberto Calasso, *K.*, translated by Geoffrey Brock, chapter VI (New York: Vintage, 2005).

RETURN OF THE PRODIGAL: Template of something vaguely remembered I'd read in Pound some forty years ago, a Chinese calendar. Actually about the return of my son from England, June 2006, after twelve years abroad. Second day of summer, June 22, also involved.

HOMAGE TO WHAT'S-HIS-NAME: For Mark Strand.

HOVERCRAFT: John McIntire, June 27, 1907.